Our Government in Action

Project Editor: William Lefkowitz / Contributing Editor: Deborah Kransberg
Copy Editor: Elaine Katz / Editorial Assistant: Carol Ann Brimeyer
Casebound Edition Editors: Carol Hegarty; Deborah Kransberg
Designer: E. Carol Gee

Production Manager: E. Carol Gee / Typesetting Administrator: Arlene Hardwick
Manufacturing Administrator: Elizabeth L. Tong

Cover Photographer: Stone & Steccati / Text Illustrator: P. L. McDonel
Typographers: Goodtype; Digitype / Printer: Murray Printing, Inc.

Our Government in Action

William Lefkowitz • Richard Uhlich

Consultant

Sherman Lewis, Ph.D.
Professor of Political Science
California State University
Hayward, California

Janus Books
Hayward, California

Acknowledgments

The authors and the publisher wish to thank the following people for their help in the development of *Our Government in Action:*

Teachers
Bernard Medeiros and Karen Taylor, Hayward (California) Unified School District; Jerrold Wisneki, Francis T. Maloney High School, Meriden, CT

City and County Officials, Middletown, CT
Michael Cubeta, Mayor; Sergeant George Keithan, Police Department; Michael Kokoszaka, Chief Clerk, Middlesex Superior Court; George Reif, Director of Planning and Zoning

Attorney at Law
Verne A. Perry, Hayward, CA

Photo Sources
AP/Wide World Photos, California Department of Transportation, Computer Election Systems, The Daily Review, Jeroboam, Inc., The National Archives, Peterbilt Motors Company, The San Francisco Examiner, The San Jose Mercury News, Santa Clara County, UPI/Bettmann Newsphotos, U.S. Army, U.S. House of Representatives, U.S. Navy
VOTE TODAY posters donated by Berkeley Citizens Action, Berkeley, California

Printed in the United States of America.

ISBN 0-88102-047-8 6 7 8 9 0 1 2 3 4 5 D—P 0 9 8 7 6 5 4 3 2

Contents

Part 1
Congress, the President, and the Courts

(continued)

Part 2
From City Hall to State Capitol

Part 1

Congress, the President, and the Courts

Introduction

Have you ever heard people say things like this?

"They ought to fix these streets!"
"They ought to stop crime!"
"They ought to do something about high prices!"

Whom do these people mean by "they"?

These people mean the **government**. They mean that the government ought to fix the streets, stop crime, and bring down high prices.

But who or what is government? Is it a building, a place, a person, a group of people?

Government is all these things.

Government is the people who make, carry out, and apply our laws. Government is the places where these people work, and the things they use to do their work.

All the people who work for the government in the United States work for you! The places where they work and the things that they use all belong to you—and to the millions of other Americans.

That's because here in the United States we have a government "of the people, for the people, by the people."

Many Americans believe that ours is the fairest kind of government in the world today. But they also know we all have to work hard to keep it fair. To do that, we have to understand how our government works, and how we can take part in what it does.

You can understand how our government works.
You can take part in the work it does.
You can help make sure it works for you.
How? Read on and find out!

unit 1

What Does Government Do?

Picture this . . .

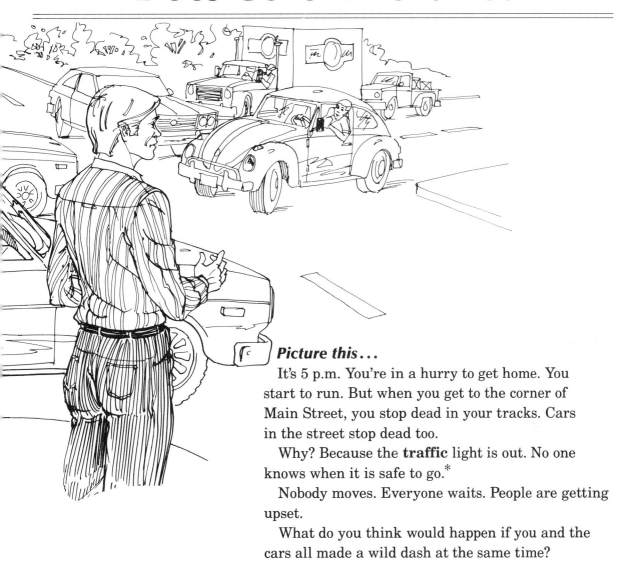

It's 5 p.m. You're in a hurry to get home. You start to run. But when you get to the corner of Main Street, you stop dead in your tracks. Cars in the street stop dead too.

Why? Because the **traffic** light is out. No one knows when it is safe to go.*

Nobody moves. Everyone waits. People are getting upset.

What do you think would happen if you and the cars all made a wild dash at the same time?

Pow! Splat! Crunch! There'd be a real mess. Right?

---

*The words that appear in dark letters in a sentence are important words you should know.

Controls Traffic

Traffic is a big problem in any town or city. Someone has to do something to **control** it. That "someone" is government.

Think a moment. What does government usually do to keep cars and people from running into each other at street corners?

If you thought, "It puts up stop signs and traffic lights," you are right. Or you might have said, "It has a **police officer** on the corner." Either way, government helps to keep people safe by controlling traffic.

What are some other ways that government controls the traffic in your town or city?

Did you think of painted lines and crosswalks, **speed limits**, and traffic signs?

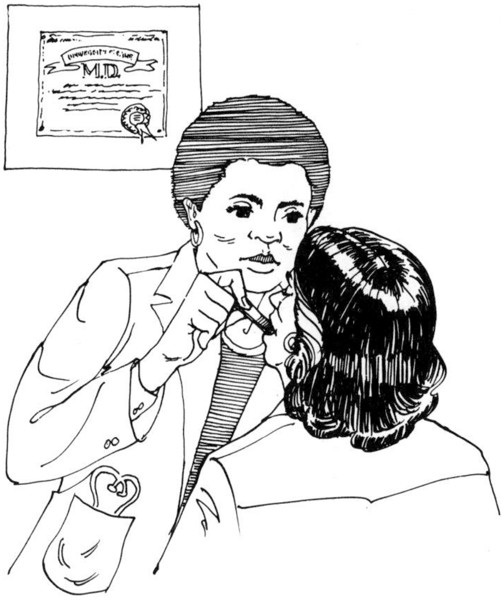

Picture this...

You have a really bad sore throat that won't go away. You can't sleep. You can't eat. You need to see a doctor.

OK. Somebody gives you the name of a doctor, and you go to see her.

But how can you find out if the doctor has the skills to take care of you?

Did you say that you can make sure she has a **license**?

Protects People

Doctors have to pass tests and get a license before they can treat people. They have to prove to the government that they have the skills to help people who are sick or hurt. This is one way the government helps to **protect** people.

Doctors aren't the only ones who have to get a license before they are allowed to do their job.

Take a look at the list below. Which of the people in the list do you think need a license?

1. Cooks
2. Dentists
3. Lawyers
4. Plumbers
5. Teachers
6. Clerks

Right. Dentists, lawyers, plumbers, and teachers need a license before they are allowed to work.

Picture this...

You live in an apartment house, and the house is on fire. You're one of the lucky ones. You get out quickly.

People on the upper floors are not so lucky. They are trapped. There is no way out. The stairs are full of smoke and fire. And the people are too high up to jump.

Whom would you call to help save the people trapped inside the building?

This is a job for the fire **department**. Right? It can **provide** the help that's needed.

Provides Important Services

In most towns and cities, fire fighters work for the government. They and the police help protect lives and **property**. Protecting lives and property is just one of the many important services that government provides.

What are some other services that government provides?

Did you think of schools, hospitals, and highways?

Picture this . . .

It's the last five seconds of a big game. The score is tied. Someone passes the ball to Ramirez.

Ramirez breaks loose and dribbles down the court. He's under the basket. He turns and leaps up to make a shot. It misses.

But wait a minute! Something's wrong! The **referee** is blowing her whistle.

What happened? The picture on this page tells the story. Why do you think the referee blew her whistle?

The referee saw player 32 hit Ramirez. That's against the rules. The referee is there to **enforce** the rules. She will let Ramirez take two free shots.

Makes and Enforces Laws

What do you think pro basketball would be like if there were no rules and no referees to enforce them?

You guessed it. There might be a lot of cheating and fighting.

The same is true in our daily lives. We all need rules to help us get along with each other.

Certain people in the government make those rules and call them **laws**. Other people in the government carry out and enforce those laws. That is, they make sure that we all **obey** the laws.

We have looked at four important things that government does. Government

- controls traffic;
- protects people;
- provides important services; and
- makes and enforces laws.

Informed Citizen

An **informed citizen** knows a lot about his or her government. You are becoming an informed citizen by reading this book. See what you've learned so far.

Facts First

Each sentence below becomes a fact when you choose the best word or words to complete it.

1. Government helps control traffic by
   a. selling fewer cars.
   b. walking more.
   c. putting up traffic lights.
2. Before doctors or dentists can treat you, they have to ask the government for
   a. money.
   b. a license.
   c. tools.
3. Schools, hospitals, and fire departments are examples of some government
   a. laws.
   b. services.
   c. people.
4. The rules that government makes for us are called
   a. controls.
   b. licenses.
   c. laws.

Beyond the Facts

Here are some questions to think and talk about.

1. How does government make sure that people know how to drive safely?
2. Suppose government did not do this. What might happen?
3. Suppose there were no government at all. How might life be different for you?

Close to Home

Here is something you might like to do. It will help you see why government is really important to you.

Make two lists like the ones below. Add as many things to each list as you can think of.

Things Government Makes Me Do

1. Pay taxes
2. Stop at red lights

Things Government Does for Me

1. Puts out fires
2. Builds roads

unit 2

Where Is Government Found?

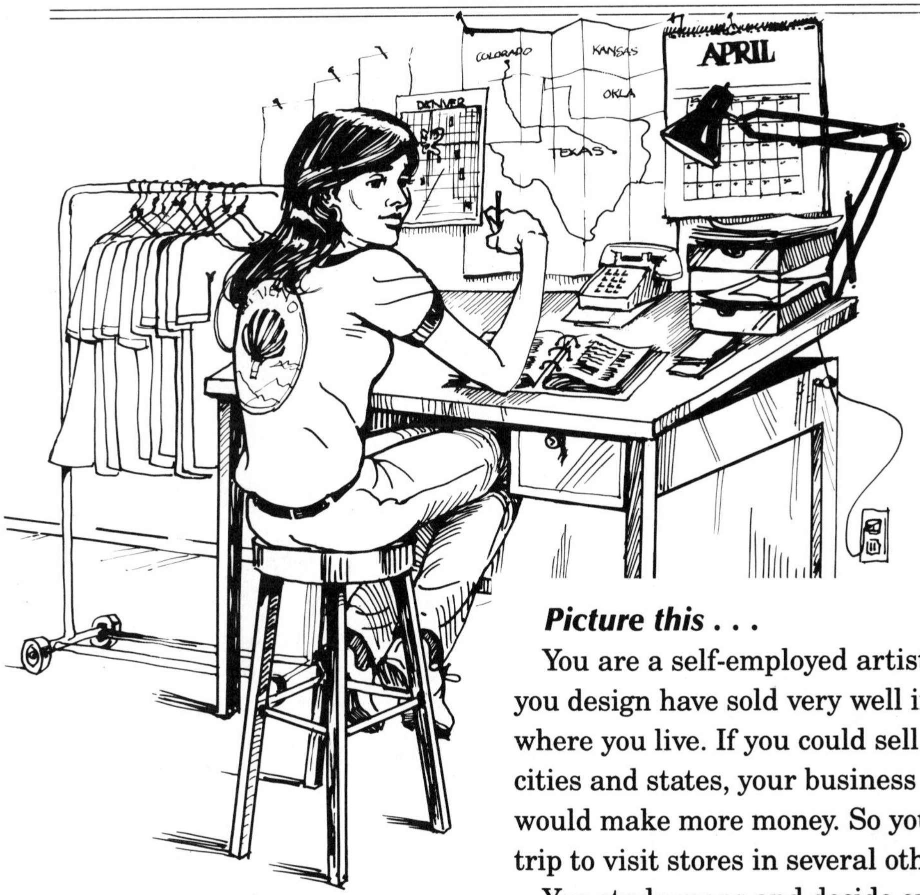

Picture this . . .

You are a self-employed artist. The T-shirts that you design have sold very well in Austin, Texas, where you live. If you could sell to stores in other cities and states, your business would grow and you would make more money. So you are planning a car trip to visit stores in several other places.

You study maps and decide on the best **national**, **state**, and **local** highways to use to get from place to place. Also, you plan to find out what laws apply to selling T-shirts in all the cities and towns you will visit. In Austin, you have to follow certain national, state, and local business laws. If there are special laws for Austin, you are sure there will be other business laws in other places.

You are glad you are not leaving for three weeks. It will take time to make phone calls, write letters, and study new information. Then you can take your T-shirts on the road!

Where Do You Live?

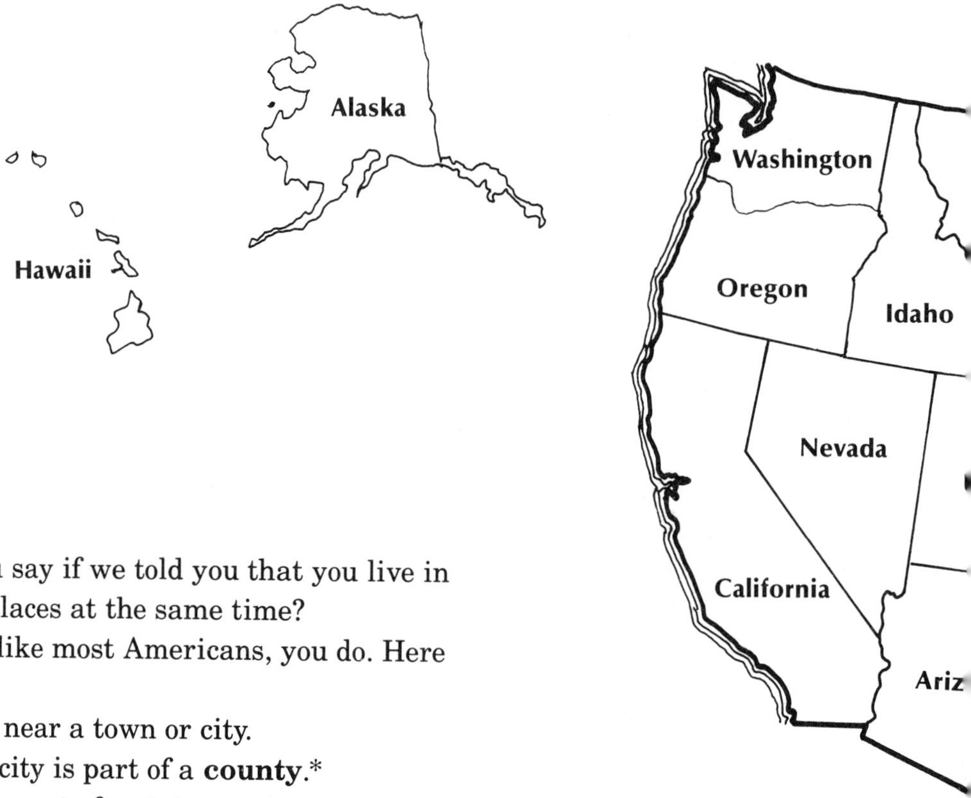

What would you say if we told you that you live in several different places at the same time?

Well, if you are like most Americans, you do. Here is what we mean.

- You live in or near a town or city.
- That town or city is part of a **county**.*
- Your county is part of a state.
- Your state is part of a **nation** called the United States of America.

What town or city do you live in or near?

What county do you live in?

What state do you live in?

---

*In some states, this is called a township, a parish, or a borough.

United States of America

What county is Austin in?

What state is that county in?

What nation is Texas in?

Three Levels of Government

Each of the places you live in has a government.

- Your town or city has a government.
- Your county has a government.
- Your state has a government.
- Your nation has a government.

These governments have different amounts of power.

- The national government has the most power.
- State governments are second in power.
- Third in power are the local governments that run counties, cities, and towns.

These three kinds of government—national, state, and local—are called the three **levels** of government.

Government workers trim stacks of newly printed dollar bills. Which level of government do you think the men work for?

National Government

The most powerful government in the United States is the national government. It makes laws for the whole nation. It prints and **coins** our money. It runs our **armed forces**. It deals with other nations.

The national government has offices and workers in every state. But its main offices are in our nation's **capital**—Washington, D.C. A capital is a city where lawmakers meet.*

State Government

A state government makes laws for all the people in that state. It makes laws about such things as driving, working, going to school, and getting married.

A state government also builds and takes care of highways. It helps people set up local governments.

A state government has offices and workers all over the state. But its main offices are in the state capital.

Why do you think each state needs a capital?

---

*The word *capitol*—with an *o*—means the building where lawmakers meet.

UPI/Bettmann Newsphotos

Local Government

When we talk about local government, we mean the governments of counties, cities, and towns. We also mean groups of people who run special **districts**, such as school, fire, or water districts.

Local government provides police and fire **protection**. It runs schools and hospitals. It builds local roads. It makes traffic and parking laws for local streets and roads. And it enforces those laws.

The people who run a town or city government usually meet in a place called a town hall or city hall. The home of a county government is usually called the county seat.

Where do the people who run your town or city and your county meet?

Here is a review of some things that national, state, and local governments do.

Three Levels of Government

National Government

- Makes laws for the whole nation
- Prints and coins money
- Runs the armed forces
- Deals with other nations
- Meets in Washington, D.C.

State Government

- Makes laws for a whole state
- Helps people set up local governments
- Builds state highways
- Meets in the state capital

Local Government

- Makes laws for counties, cities, and towns
- Enforces local traffic and parking laws
- Provides police and fire protection, schools, roads, and hospitals
- May meet in town hall, city hall, and the county seat

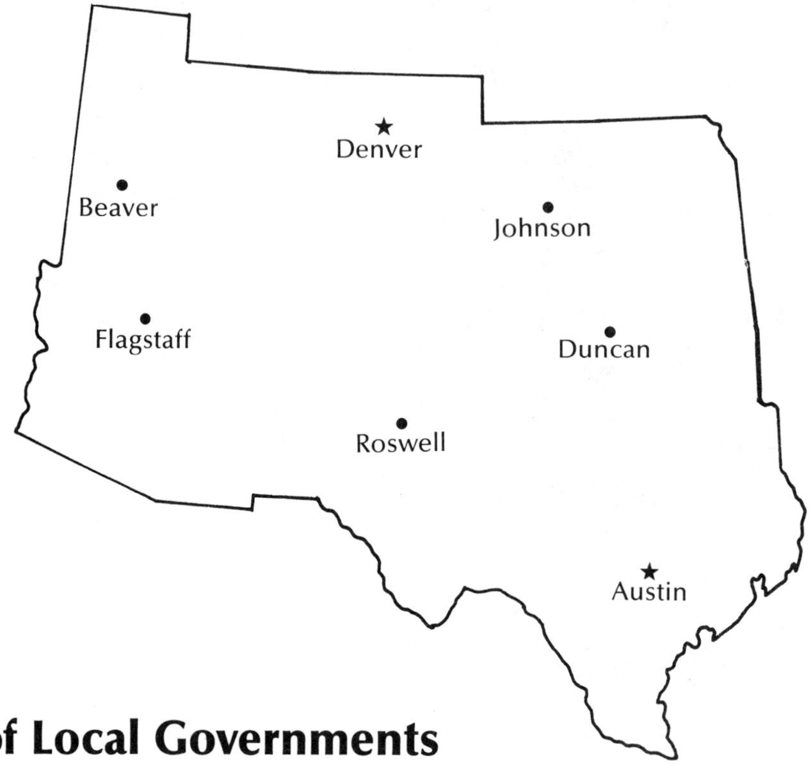

Thousands of Local Governments

Look at the map. It shows seven towns and cities you might visit on a trip to the western part of the United States.

The map shows only seven places. But there are hundreds more in this part of the United States. And there are many thousands more in the rest of the country. Each town or city has some form of government to handle local matters.

Look under *Local Government* on the chart on page 19. This list shows some important things that local government does. Other things include giving people **permits** to build houses and office buildings. Local government also collects local **taxes** and uses the money to pay its bills. Water and sewer services are local matters, too.

What is the name of your town or city?

Where do the people who run your local government meet?

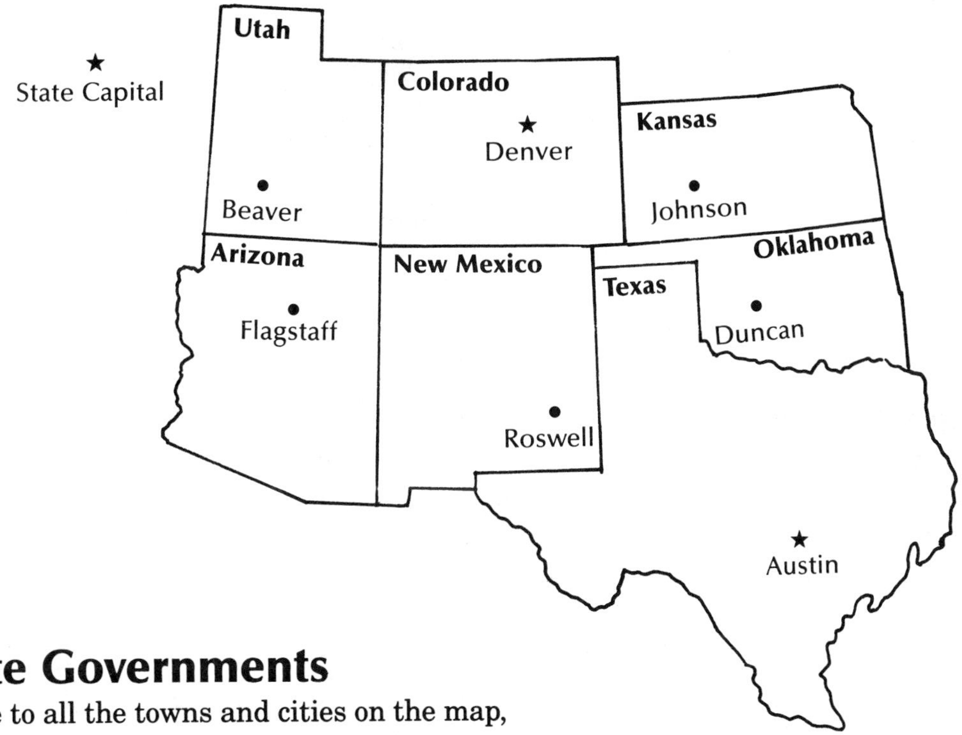

Fifty State Governments

If you drove to all the towns and cities on the map, you would drive through seven states. All together, there are 50 states in the United States of America. Each of those 50 states has a state government.

On page 19, find the list of *State Government* activities on the chart. Only a few things states do are listed there. Others include taking care of state highways, as well as testing drivers and giving out driver's licenses. State government helps people who are out of work. It makes special laws for businesses. State government also collects state taxes and uses the money to help pay the state's bills.

Two of the cities shown on the map are state capitals. Each of those cities has a star next to its name.

What is the capital of Texas? What is the capital of Colorado?

Austin is the capital of Texas. Denver is the capital of Colorado.

What is the name of your state? And what is its capital?

One United States of America

All 50 states together make up one nation, or country, called the United States of America. Look at the map of the United States on pages 16 and 17. It shows and names all 50 states. Find your state. Which states are your neighbors?

Our Nation's Capital

Look at the list under *National Government* on page 19. You will see that the national government meets in Washington, D.C., the capital of our nation. National laws are made in this capital. Some national laws help people in one state do business with people in other states. Other national laws help people and businesses in the United States work with the rest of the world. Our national government builds superhighways for fast travel from one end of the country to another. It develops and maintains the national parks. It uses the taxes it collects to pay some of the costs of its work and its services.

The important jobs of national government are directed from Washington, D.C. But national government offices are located throughout the United States. This means we can work with our national government without going to Washington.

Not Part of Any State

Look at the map on pages 16 and 17. What state do you think Washington, D.C., is in?

It is not in any state! Washington, D.C., is the only city in the United States that is not part of any state.

Why? Because the people who set up the national government could not agree on which state our nation's capital should be in. So they said it should have its own land, or district. D.C. stands for **District of Columbia**. The district was located on land between the states of Maryland and Virginia. And that's still where it is today.

Informed Citizen

Facts First

Choose the right word from the Word List to complete each sentence below.

Word List

state	Washington, D.C.
levels	local
capital	national

1. In the United States, we have three ________________ of government.
2. When we talk about ________________ governments, we mean the governments of counties, cities, and towns.
3. You have to get your driver's license from your ________________ government.
4. Money is printed and coined by the ________________ government.
5. A city where people meet to make laws is called a ________________.
6. The capital of the United States is ________________ .

Beyond the Facts

Here are some questions to think and talk about.

1. Who do you think should set speed limits on city streets—local, state, or national government? Why?
2. Who do you think should build and take care of highways that go all over the state—local, state, or national government? Why?
3. Who do you think should print and coin money—local, state, or national government? Why?

Close to Home

Here are some things you might like to do.

1. On a separate piece of paper, write out your full address. Put each fact on a different line:
   Street address
   Town or city
   County or similar place
   State
   Nation

   Compare your facts with your classmates. Who lives closest to you? Who lives farthest away? Use a map.
2. Make a scrapbook with different parts for local, state, and national news. Clip stories from newspapers and magazines and put them where they belong in the scrapbook. Talk about these news stories with classmates.

unit 3

Who Set Up Our Government?

Today you can travel from state to state with no problems. But it wasn't always that way. Back about 200 years ago, things were quite different.

Picture this . . .

The time is about 200 years ago.

You are living in the state of Maryland.

You want to travel to the city of Philadelphia in the state of Pennsylvania. You have to go there to buy some tea, gunpowder, and other things you need.

While you are in Philadelphia, you want to visit some friends. You pack your saddlebags with gifts of homemade soap and candles.

At the state line, where you leave Maryland and enter Pennsylvania, a **tax collector** stops you. He searches your saddlebags.

"You will have to pay a tax on these gifts," the tax collector says. "The money goes to the government of Pennsylvania."

"The government of Pennsylvania!" you shout. "Why should I pay money to the government of Pennsylvania?"

"Pay the money or turn back," the tax collector says.

You're really upset, but you pay the money and move on.

In Philadelphia, you go to a shop to buy some tea. You want to pay for the tea with Maryland money. But the shopkeeper says, "We only take Pennsylvania money here!" You walk out without your tea.

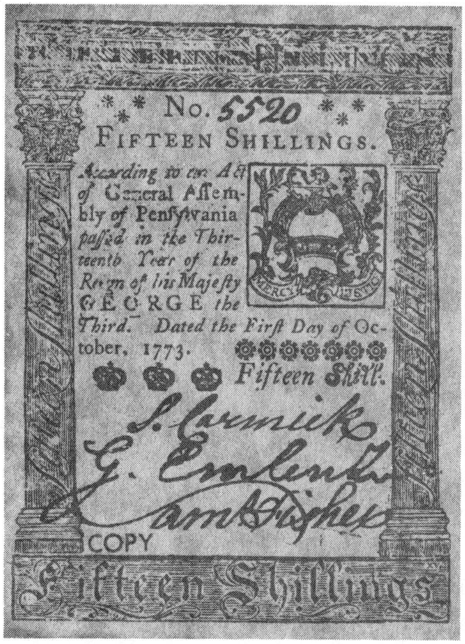

Pennsylvania money (1773)

Could It Have Happened?

Do you think these things could have happened if you were living 200 years ago?

Yes, they could have. Because in those days there were only 13 states. Each state was like a separate country, with its own laws and money. And many states did not get along with each other.

There was a national government too. But it was very weak. It did not have the power to make the states obey its laws.

In 1787, however, things began to change.

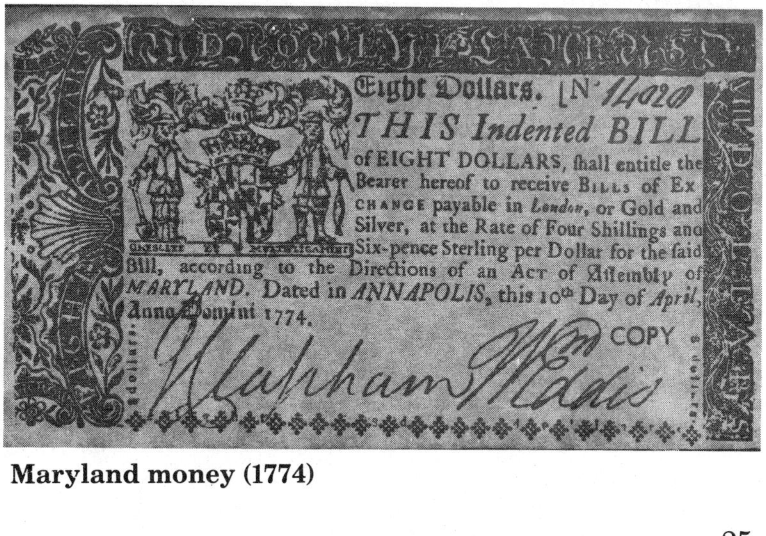

Maryland money (1774)

Important people from different states met in Philadelphia to plan a new national government. Can you name the two men whose faces are circled?

Meeting in Philadelphia

In 1787, the United States of America was only a few years old. And it wasn't very *united*!

That was only a few years after the states had won their freedom from England. The states had not yet learned how to form a strong, united nation.

Leaders in some of the states were worried that the new United States wouldn't last. They were afraid that each state would end up being a small country. Then stronger countries, such as England or Spain, might come in and take over each one.

Leaders Call Meeting

These leaders called for a meeting of important people from all the states. They wanted the people to make up a plan for a new national government—one that would help keep the states together and strong.

In May of 1787, **delegates** from 12 of the 13 states met in Philadelphia. A delegate is someone who is chosen by a group of people to speak for them at a meeting. Rhode Island refused to send any delegates. It didn't want any changes in the national government.

George Washington headed the meeting. Another famous person at the meeting was Benjamin Franklin.

Washington was a great leader. Franklin was very wise. It took all of Washington's strong leadership and Franklin's wisdom to get the delegates to agree on anything.

First Thirteen States

The National Archives

Lots of Fighting

The meeting lasted from May to September—four long, hot months. The delegates talked and fought about what to do. Often, the talks became shouting matches.

Some of the delegates did not want a strong national government to rule over the states.

"We just fought a war to be free from English rule," said one of the delegates. "We don't want someone else now to tell us what we can and cannot do."

But another delegate said, "We need a strong national government to keep one state from making laws that hurt another state. And we need a strong national government to fight for us if we are attacked by England or Spain."

Suppose you were one of the delegates at the meeting. Which of the following would you vote for?

1. Strong state governments; weak national government
2. Strong national government; no state governments
3. Strong state governments; but even stronger national government

In the end, the delegates agreed to keep the strong state governments, but to make the national government even stronger than the states. This kind of government is called a **federal** government. Sometimes when we are talking about the national government, we call it the federal government.

We the People of the United States, in Order to form a more perfect Union, establish Justice, insure domestic Tranquility, provide for the common defence, promote the general Welfare, and secure the Blessings of Liberty to ourselves and our Posterity, do ordain and establish this Constitution for the United States of America.

Article. I.

Section. 1. All legislative Powers herein granted shall be vested in a Congress of the United States, which shall consist of a Senate and House of Representatives.

Section. 2. The House of Representatives shall be composed of Members chosen every second Year by the People of the several States, and the Electors in each State shall have the Qualifications requisite for Electors of the most numerous Branch of the State Legislature.

No Person shall be a Representative who shall not have attained to the Age of twenty five Years, and been seven Years a Citizen of the United States, and who shall not, when elected, be an Inhabitant of that State in which he shall be chosen.

Representatives and direct Taxes shall be apportioned among the several States which may be included within this Union, according to their respective Numbers, which shall be determined by adding to the whole Number of free Persons, including those bound to Service for a Term of Years, and excluding Indians not taxed, three fifths of all other Persons. The actual Enumeration shall be made within three Years after the first Meeting of the Congress of the United States, and within every subsequent Term of ten Years, in such Manner as they shall by Law direct. The Number of Representatives shall not exceed one for every thirty Thousand, but each State shall have at Least one Representative; and until such enumeration shall be made, the State of New Hampshire shall be entitled to chuse three, Massachusetts eight, Rhode Island and Providence Plantations one, Connecticut five, New York six, New Jersey four, Pennsylvania eight, Delaware one, Maryland six, Virginia ten, North Carolina five, South Carolina five, and Georgia three.

When vacancies happen in the Representation from any State, the Executive Authority thereof shall issue Writs of Election to fill such Vacancies.

The House of Representatives shall chuse their Speaker and other Officers; and shall have the sole Power of Impeachment.

Section. 3. The Senate of the United States shall be composed of two Senators from each State, chosen by the Legislature thereof for six Years; and each Senator shall have one Vote.

Immediately after they shall be assembled in Consequence of the first Election, they shall be divided as equally as may be into three Classes. The Seats of the Senators of the first Class shall be vacated at the Expiration of the second Year, of the second Class at the Expiration of the fou[illegible] the third Class at the Expiration of the sixth Year, so that one third may be chos[illegible] Vacancies happen by [illegible]

Here is the opening of the Constitution and some of the first article.

Plan for Government

Once the delegates finally agreed on what to do, they wrote a plan for the new federal government. They called their plan the **Constitution of the United States**.

A constitution is a plan for government. It tells how the laws are to be made and carried out, and by whom.

A constitution may also tell what **powers** the government has. That is, it may tell what the government can and cannot do.

Some constitutions also tell what **rights** the people have. But the delegates didn't put a list of the people's rights in the U.S. Constitution. It wasn't added until later.

The Constitution of the United States has seven parts. Each part is called an **article**.

Informed Citizen

Facts First

Choose the best word or words to complete each sentence below.

1. Before 1787, the national government in America was
   a. strong.
   b. weak.
   c. unfair.
2. Delegates from different states met in Philadelphia to plan for a
   a. war with England.
   b. new state government.
   c. new national government.
3. The delegates agreed to
   a. do away with the national government.
   b. make the national government stronger.
   c. do away with state governments.
4. The delegates wrote a plan for government called a
   a. tax.
   b. court.
   c. constitution.
5. The delegates did not write anything in the Constitution about
   a. how government is set up.
   b. people's rights.
   c. how to add new laws.
6. Another name for the national government is the
   a. federal government.
   b. state government.
   c. local government.

Beyond the Facts

Here are some questions to think and talk about.

1. If you were going to send a delegate to speak for you at an important meeting, what kind of person would you want that delegate to be?
2. What do you think it takes to be a good leader of a group meeting?
3. What are some things the leader of a group must do to help members of the group reach some agreement? What must the members be willing to do?

Close to Home

Here is something you might like to do.

Write a constitution for your class or club. Talk over this idea with classmates or friends. Pick a leader to run the meeting. Talk about these things:

- Why might a constitution be helpful?
- What should the constitution tell?
- Who should decide what goes into the constitution?
- Who should write it?
- How will you make sure everyone obeys it?

After you read the next unit in this book, you will have a better idea of some of the things that you might put into your constitution.

unit 4

How Is Power Kept in Check?

HOUSE RULES
1. NO LOUD MUSIC
2. NO PETS
3. NO PARTIES
4. NO VISITORS
5. LIGHTS OUT BY 10:00PM
6. ROOMS MUST BE CLEANED DAILY.

Picture this...

You have been living in your own place for a few years. You're used to doing what you want to do, when you want to do it.

But your rent is high, and there has been a lot of crime lately. You're afraid of being robbed and beaten. So you're thinking of moving in with some other people. It will be cheaper and safer for you.

But those people want to set up rules about what you can and cannot do in the house. And they want one strong person or group to enforce the rules.

Would you be willing to give up some of your freedom in order to save money and feel safer?

The National Archives

Some delegates were afraid of losing their freedom.

Delegates Fear Super-Government

The delegates in Philadelphia had a similar question to answer. As long as the national government was weak, state governments had a lot of freedom. Many delegates were afraid that a strong national government would cut down on some of that freedom.

Other delegates were willing to give up some freedom in order to make things better between the states. And to get protection against attack.

But the delegates were afraid of giving too much power to any one person or group. That would be too much like the days when they were ruled by the king of England.

Power Split Three Ways

The delegates decided to **separate** the powers of the new federal government. That way, no one could ever have as much power over them as the king of England once had.

The delegates decided to split the powers of government among three groups of people.

- One group would make the laws.
- Another group would carry out and enforce the laws.
- A third group would hold **trials**, settle **disputes**, and decide if the laws were fair.

Three Branches

Today, we call each of the three groups a **branch** of government. There is a **legislative** branch, an **executive** branch, and a **judicial** branch.

The delegates wrote in the Constitution what they wanted each branch to do. Read on and find out what they had in mind.

This is the chamber, or big room, where the House of Representatives meets. The Senate meets in a similar chamber.

Here is what the Constitution says about the three branches. We have made the language easier to read.

Article 1: Legislative Branch

The legislative branch will make laws for the nation. The group that makes the laws will be called the **Congress**. The Congress will have two houses: a **House of Representatives**, and a **Senate**. The Congress will meet at least once a year.

The House of Representatives

To become a member of the House of Representatives, a person must be at least 25 years old. The person must have been a citizen of the United States for seven years, and must live in the state in which he or she is chosen.

Members are to be chosen from each of the states every second year. They are called **representatives**.

The Senate

To become a member of the Senate, a person must be at least 30 years old. The person must have been a citizen of the United States for nine years, and must live in the state in which he or she is chosen.

Each state may choose two members. The members will serve for six years. They are called **senators**.

UPI/Bettmann Newsphotos

Passing a Law

Any laws that the Congress wants must be approved and signed by the President of the United States. If the President does not approve and sign a law, the Congress may vote on it again. If **two-thirds** of those present in each house vote for the law, then it will become law without the President signing it.

Powers of the Congress

The Congress may

1. Collect taxes and borrow money to pay the costs of government.
2. Control trade with other nations and between states.
3. Coin and print money.
4. Set up post offices.
5. Form armies and navies.
6. Declare war on other nations.

Checks on the Powers of the Congress

The Congress may not

1. Take away the people's right to a speedy trial if they are arrested, unless the nation is in great danger.
2. Collect a tax on goods moved from one state to another.
3. Favor trade in one state over that in another.
4. Spend any money that has not been approved by law.

Article 2: Executive Branch

The executive branch will be headed by a President. The President will be elected by people from all the states for a four-year term. He or she must be at least 35 years old and must have been born in the United States.

Before taking over as President, the person must promise to "**preserve**, protect, and **defend** the Constitution of the United States."

President Reagan reports to the Congress about how the country is doing.

United States House of Representatives

Powers of the President

The President:

1. Is chief of the armed forces.
2. Is head of all departments that carry out and enforce U.S. laws.
3. May make **treaties** (agreements) with other nations.
4. May appoint people to high jobs in U.S. government.

Duties of the President

The President will

1. Make sure that federal laws are carried out and enforced.
2. Report to the Congress about how the country is doing.
3. Suggest ways to solve the nation's problems.

Checks on the President's Powers

If found guilty of wrongdoing, the President may be removed from office by the Congress.

Article 3: Judicial Branch

The power to hear and decide **cases of law** belongs to the judicial branch. Trials for all **crimes** will be by **jury** (except for the trial of a President or other high government officer).

Informed Citizen

Facts First

Match each job on the left with the branch of government that does that job.

1. Carries out and enforces laws
2. Hear and decide cases of law
3. Makes federal laws

a. The courts
b. The Congress
c. The President

4. Makes a law about the taxes people must pay
5. Makes sure that the law is obeyed
6. Hold the trials of people who are arrested for not paying their taxes

d. The President
e. The courts
f. The Congress

Beyond the Facts

Here are some questions to think and talk about.

1. Why do you suppose people have to be a certain age before they can become members of the Congress or President of the United States?
2. The President must promise to "preserve, protect, and defend the Constitution of the United States." What do you think that promise means, and why is it necessary?
3. Do you think it is a good idea to separate the powers of government? Why or why not?

Close to Home

Here are some things you might like to do.

1. Are you working on a class or club constitution? If you are, you may want to list the powers of your officers the way the U.S. Constitution does. (See pages 33 and 34.)
2. Find out about the three branches of your local government.
   - Who makes local laws?
   - Who carries out and enforces those laws?
   - Who hears and decides cases of law?

unit 5

What Are the People's Rights?

Picture this...

You're sitting in your kitchen with a friend, after looking for work all day.

"Sure is tough out there," says your friend. "I think the government is messing up real bad. That's why there are no jobs."

"That's what I think too," you say. "Fact is, that's just what I told someone today. I said..."

Suddenly your front door bangs open. A soldier rushes in.

"Hands up!" the soldier shouts. "You are **under arrest** for speaking against the government."

Do you think this could happen in the United States today?

No, it couldn't. Soldiers are not allowed to break into your home or arrest you for speaking against the government. You are protected from such things by the **Bill of Rights**. The Bill of Rights is a part of the Constitution.

Rights Were Added Later

At first, the Constitution didn't say enough about people's rights. That made a lot of Americans angry. They said such things as:

> There's nothing in this Constitution to protect us. The national government could throw us in jail for anything—and keep us there forever!

For a while, it looked as though many Americans would not accept the Constitution. If it was not accepted in at least nine of the states, it could not become law.

The delegates found an answer to the problem. What do you suppose they did?

Delegates Make a Promise

The delegates promised that as soon as the first Congress met, it would add a list of rights to the Constitution.

These rights would become the first **amendments** to the Constitution. An amendment is any law added to the Constitution after the Constitution has been accepted.

The promise of the delegates seemed to satisfy most people. They finally accepted the Constitution, even though it did not list their rights.

First Ten Amendments

In 1791, the people got their rights. Those rights were listed in the first ten amendments to the Constitution. These ten amendments became known as the Bill of Rights because they told about the people's rights.

The Bill of Rights was written almost 200 years ago. But it still protects you and all Americans from unfair government. How? Read on and find out.

The San Francisco Examiner

The First Amendment gives Americans the right to assemble and to speak out for what they want.

All About Freedom

The First Amendment to the Constitution is all about freedom. It says that Americans have the right to four freedoms. These freedoms are described below.

First Amendment

1. **Freedom of Religion**
   The government may not force you to follow one **religion** or another. It may not stop you from following the religion of your choice.

2. **Freedom of Speech**
   The government may not keep you from making a **speech** about it or from saying what you think about it.

3. **Freedom of the Press**
   The government may not tell reporters and other members of the **press** what news they may or may not report.

4. **Freedom of Assembly**
   You have the right to **assemble** with other people and talk about the government, or to ask the government to do something, as long as your meeting is peaceful.

If You Are Arrested

The Fourth, Fifth, Sixth, and Eighth Amendments are about being arrested. Here is how they protect you.

Fourth Amendment

The police must have a good reason to believe that you have broken a law before they may search your home or arrest you. Even then, unless they catch you breaking a law, they must first get a **warrant** from the courts. A warrant is a piece of paper that says the police may search your home or may arrest you.

UPI/Bettmann Newsphotos

The man on the left has been arrested. What rights do you think he has, if any?

Fifth Amendment

If you are arrested, you do not have to say anything that might make you seem **guilty**. Once you are on trial, you do not have to answer any question if you think your answer might make you seem guilty. If the court allows you to go free, you may not be arrested again for the same crime.

Sixth Amendment

If you are arrested, the police must tell you why they are arresting you. They must let you have a **lawyer**. And the government must give you a trial as soon as possible.

Eighth Amendment

Judges may not set **bail** at an amount too high for anyone to pay. Bail is money an accused person pays the court as a promise that he or she will appear for trial.

Judges may not set fines that are unreasonable. And they may not call for cruel or unusual punishment.

Five Other Amendments

Here are the other five amendments that are part of the Bill of Rights. Some of these amendments were very important to Americans at the time they were written. They may seem less important today. Which of the amendments do you think are still important?

Second Amendment

Since people may be called upon to help protect the country, the government may not keep people from owning guns.

Third Amendment

In time of peace, the government may not put soldiers in people's homes without permission from the people. If the government needs places for soldiers in wartime, it must pass a special law. The law would say that people must take soldiers into their homes.

If the army asked you to give these soldiers a place to stay, would you have to do it?

© Bob Clay/Jeroboam, Inc.

Seventh Amendment

In court cases involving amounts of $20 or more, the people involved have the right to a trial by jury.

Ninth Amendment

Government may not take away other rights of the people just because those rights aren't listed in the Constitution.

Tenth Amendment

All those powers not listed in the Constitution as belonging to the federal government belong to the state governments or to the people.

Informed Citizen

Facts First

Choose the right word or words from the Word List to complete each sentence below.

Word List

amendments	Bill of Rights
search	arrested
freedoms	rights

1. At first, the Constitution did not say anything about the people's ________________.
2. Later, the first Congress added the first ten ________________ to the Constitution.
3. The first ten amendments are also known as the ________________ .
4. The First Amendment tells about four ________________ .
5. The Fourth Amendment says the police must have a warrant before they may ________________ your home.
6. The Fifth and Sixth Amendments tell what your rights are if you are ________________ .

Beyond the Facts

Here are some questions to think and talk about.

1. Freedom of speech is one of the most important rights we have in the United States. Why?
2. Do you think freedom of speech means you can say anything you like, anytime, anywhere? Why or why not?
3. What do you think is a wise use of the right to free speech? What is not a wise use of that right?

Close to Home

Here are some things you might like to do.

1. If you are working on a constitution, add a bill of rights. First decide what rights class or club members ought to have. Then decide how many people in the class or the club must favor each right before it can become "law."
2. Start looking and listening for news stories about people's rights. Cut out the stories you see in newspapers and add them to your scrapbook. Talk about these stories with classmates, family, and friends.

unit 6

What Makes a Democracy?

Picture this . . .

You belong to a club. The leader is big, strong, and smart. That's how he got to be leader, by outfighting and outsmarting everyone else. The leader tells you what to do, and you do it—or else!

Or else what? Well, maybe you have to pay a fine. Or maybe you get kicked out of the club. Or maybe you even get beaten up.

Are there clubs like this? Sure. There are clubs where the strongest person, or best fighter, or smartest person takes over.

Now picture this . . .

You belong to a different club. It is run by three people who are chosen each year by the members of the club.

This club has a written constitution. It tells what the leaders may and may not do.

Are there clubs like this? Sure.

Which of the two clubs would you rather belong to, the first or the second? Why?

Shared and Limited Power

Governments can be like those two clubs. In some governments, one person or one small group of people have all the power. They control the laws, the police, the army, and the courts.

Other governments are more like the second club. People choose their leaders and lawmakers. The power of those leaders and lawmakers is limited. And the people's rights are protected.

Is the government of the United States more like the first club or the second?

Our government is more like the second club.

- We choose our leaders and lawmakers.
- Their power is limited.
- Our rights are protected.

Our kind of government is called a **democracy**. *Democracy* means rule by the people.

Direct Democracy

There are two kinds of democracy. One is **direct** democracy. That's where people get together and make all the laws and decisions. For example, in some very small towns, all the **voters** meet in one place at one time. They make laws and choose leaders.

Representative Democracy

What if all the voters can't get together in one place at one time? Then we have a second kind of democracy, called representative democracy. A representative is any person who speaks for one or more other people.

Except in very small towns, we can't all get together to make our laws. So we send representatives to do it for us. The people in Congress are our representatives.

Making Democracy Work

The people who wrote the Constitution and the Bill of Rights made a good plan for a democracy. That plan has worked for about 200 years. In order for it to keep working, certain things have to keep on happening. Here are some of those things.

UPI/Bettmann Newsphotos

Why do you think elections are important in a democracy?

Free Elections

The government must hold **elections**. The main purpose of these elections is to give people the chance to choose leaders and lawmakers. The people must also be able to get rid of leaders or lawmakers who do not do a good job, or who misuse their power.

Freedom of Speech, Press, and Assembly

In order for democracy to work, people must be free to make choices. And in order to make *wise* choices, they must be well informed. People must be able to

- find out what's going on in government;
- meet and talk about government;
- speak freely about the government; and
- bring about change in peaceful ways.

Majority Rule

The laws of the land must be acceptable to the **majority** of the people. *Majority* means more than half.

For example, for a new law to be passed by Congress, more than half of the people who vote that day in Congress must be in favor of the law.

The San Francisco Examiner

In a democracy, a minority group should have the same rights as the majority. What can a minority group do if it is not getting all its rights?

Minority Rights

A nation like the United States has many different kinds of people and different groups of people. There are people of different races and religions, young and old, rich and poor, workers and owners, and so on.

In a democracy, the rights of all these people must be protected. The largest group, the majority, cannot take away the rights of any small group, or **minority**.

Shared Power

In a democracy, power must be shared. It cannot all be in the hands of one person or group. For example, in the United States, power is shared in two ways.

- Power is shared by three levels of government—local, state, and national.
- Power is shared by three branches of government—the Congress, the President, and the courts.

A Constitution

In a democracy, there must be a set of laws—a constitution—that tells what the government is supposed to do and what it may not do. The constitution must also tell how the laws are to be made, and how they are to be carried out and enforced.

Does the U.S. Pass the Test?

Now you know six important things that are needed to keep our democracy working. Decide if the United States has those things today. If you are not sure, try to find out by talking with classmates, friends, and relatives.

1. Can Americans choose their leaders and lawmakers?
   a. Yes
   b. No
   c. Not sure
2. Do Americans have freedom of speech, press, and assembly?
   a. Yes
   b. No
   c. Not sure
3. Does a majority of Congress have to be in favor of a law before it can become the law of the land?
   a. Yes
   b. No
   c. Not sure
4. Do minority groups have the same rights as the majority of Americans?
   a. Yes
   b. No
   c. Not sure
5. Is power shared by different levels and branches of government?
   a. Yes
   b. No
   c. Not sure
6. Does the United States have a written constitution?
   a. Yes
   b. No
   c. Not sure
7. Does the United States have the six important things needed to make democracy work?
   a. Yes
   b. No
   c. Not sure

Informed Citizen

Facts First

Choose the best word or words to complete each sentence below.

1. A government that is set up to help people rule themselves is called a
   a. constitution.
   b. city hall.
   c. democracy.
2. In order to let people choose leaders and lawmakers, the government must hold
   a. taxes.
   b. meetings.
   c. elections.
3. An important reason for freedom of speech, press, and assembly is so people can
   a. enjoy themselves.
   b. make wise choices.
   c. make a lot of money.
4. In a democracy, a new law cannot be passed unless it is approved by
   a. a minority of the lawmakers.
   b. an important leader.
   c. a majority of the lawmakers.
5. In a democracy, the powers and limits of government must be written down in a
   a. constitution.
   b. report.
   c. license.

Beyond the Facts

Here are some questions to think and talk about.

1. What are some things a government must do in order to be a democracy?
2. Do you think any of the following can be run like a democracy? Why or why not?
   - A family
   - A class
   - A club
   - A school

Close to Home

Here are some things you might like to do.

1. Think about the groups you belong to—such as your class, school, club, family, or place of work.
   - In which way is each group like a democracy?
   - In which way is each group not like a democracy?
   - Are there any changes you would like to see?
   - How could you help bring about those changes?
2. Suppose you wanted to help bring about changes in a group that you belong to. Prepare a short speech. Tell what you think is wrong and what changes you would like to see. Write or record the speech.

unit 7

How Do People Get Elected?

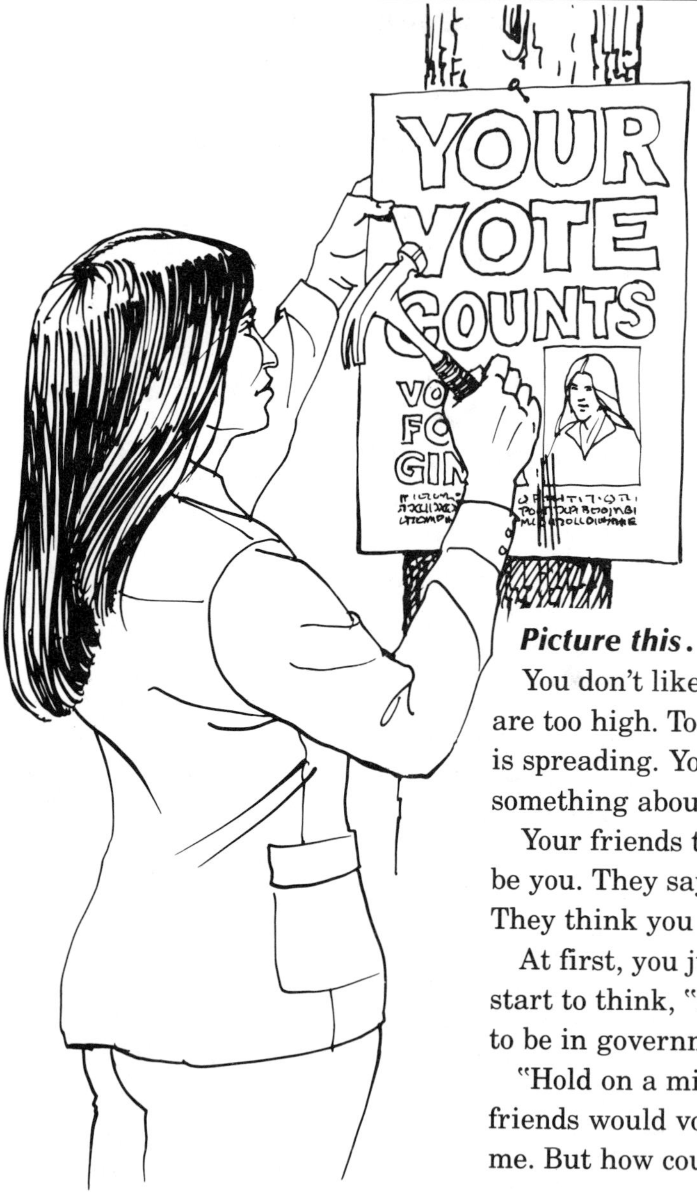

Picture this . . .

You don't like the way things are going. Prices are too high. Too many people are out of work. Crime is spreading. You think it's high time somebody did something about all this.

Your friends think maybe that "somebody" should be you. They say you ought to be in the government. They think you ought to run for Congress.

At first, you just laugh at the idea. But then you start to think, "Maybe they are right. Maybe I ought to be in government."

"Hold on a minute," you say to yourself. "My friends would vote for me. My family would vote for me. But how could I get other people to vote for me?"

Do you know the answer to that question? Do you know how people get **elected** to public office? Read on and find out.

Political Parties Help

To win an election, a person usually needs the help of a **political party**. A political party is a group of people who work to get leaders and lawmakers elected to **public office**.

In the United States, the two biggest political parties are the Democrats and the Republicans. They each have thousands of members in every state.

Which party does each animal stand for? The donkey stands for the Democrats. The elephant stands for the Republicans.

Anyone Can Join

Anyone can be a member of a party. But most of the party's work is done by a small group of people.

These people want to help elect lawmakers who will make the kinds of laws the people think are needed. And they want to help elect leaders who will run the government the way the people think it should be run.

Both Democrats and Republicans believe in the Constitution and the Bill of Rights. But they often have different ideas about what needs to be done.

Different Ideas

One party may believe that government should spend more money to help people who are out of work. The other party might believe that government should help business first, because better business means more jobs.

Which party would you agree with:

1. The party that says help the people who are out of work?
2. The party that says help business first?

The San Francisco Examiner/Chris Hardy

In 1984, Republicans met in Dallas. They chose the same candidates for President and *Vice-President* as they did in 1980. The Republicans wanted the same leaders for the next four years.

Becoming a Candidate

Let's say you decide to join a political party. So you find out what each party believes in. Then you choose the party whose beliefs seem closest to yours.

You become a member of that party, and you work in the small group of people who do most of the party's work.

Your friends know you belong to a political party, and they think you should be in the government. You think it over and decide you'd like to become a member of Congress.

You can try to get yourself elected, but that's usually pretty hard to do. A better way is to have your political party help you get elected.

First, you have to get your party to name you as its **candidate**. A candidate is a person who is running for public office.

But there may be other people in the party who also want to be the candidate. How would the party choose between you and the others? In one of two ways.

AP/Wide World Photos

Walter Mondale and Geraldine Ferraro were the Democratic candidates in 1984. Ms. Ferraro was the first woman ever to run for Vice-President. Although her party did not get elected, she made history by trying for a higher public office than any woman before her.

UPI/Bettmann Archive

Political Conventions

Sometimes a party holds a **convention**. A convention is a big meeting.

The party chooses delegates to attend the meeting. The delegates listen to speeches by and about people who want to run for each public office. Finally, the delegates vote and choose the person they think will make the best candidate for each office.

Primary Elections

Sometimes a party holds a **primary election**. The party lists the names of all the possible candidates on a **ballot**. Then party members are given a chance to mark their choice on a copy of the ballot. Whoever gets the most votes becomes the party's candidate.

Winning Votes

Becoming your party's candidate is only the first step to getting elected. Next, you have to get people to vote for you on election day.

Candidates talk to people on the streets, at places of work, and in other public places. They make speeches at meetings and on radio and TV.

The candidates tell about the good things they have done, and what they will do if elected. They may also tell why they think they would do a better job than anyone else.

AP/Wide World Photos

Making posters for a candidate

Party Workers Help

Party workers help the candidates win votes. They write and mail letters about the candidates. They put up posters, and give out balloons, buttons, and bumper stickers that tell something about the candidates.

Party workers also raise the money to pay for all this. Getting elected can cost thousands, even millions, of dollars!

Election Day

On the day that elections are held, voting machines are set up in schools, firehouses, and other places. Voters come and choose the candidate they want to see in each office.

Sometimes voters choose their own party's candidate. But sometimes they choose a candidate from another party who they think may do a better job. No one can tell whom they choose. Their vote is secret.

Finally the voting places close. The votes are counted. The candidate with the most votes wins.

Informed Citizen

Facts First

Decide if each statement below is true or false. If you think it is false, be ready to tell why you think so.

True or False

1. Political parties help people get elected.
2. The two biggest political parties in the United States are the Democrats and the Republicans.
3. A political convention is a big party for people who win elections.
4. Only party leaders can take part in choosing a party's candidates for public office.
5. A primary election is one in which people mark a ballot to show their choice for a party's candidate.
6. Party workers help raise the money that a candidate needs for posters, balloons, buttons, bumper stickers, and other things.
7. At election time, voters must vote for their party's candidate.
8. Voters must tell whom they voted for.

Beyond the Facts

Here are some questions to think and talk about.

1. Why do you suppose people want to be elected to a public office?
2. If someone doesn't have much money, could he or she still get elected? If so, how?
3. Not everyone has what it takes to be in government. But everyone can still help to shape government by doing work for a political party. What kind of work could *you* do? Which party would you want to work for?

Close to Home

Here is something you might like to do.

Form two parties in your own class. Decide what each party stands for. For example, one party might want strict rules, while the other party might want more freedom.

Decide what to call each party. Then get ready for an election, perhaps to choose a class president. First, each party chooses a candidate. Then each party helps its candidate win votes.

Finally, hold an election.

unit 8

How Does Congress Work?

Picture this...

You ran for Congress and won! You are now one of the 435 members of the House of Representatives.

You live in Washington, D.C. Every morning, you start your busy day by watching the news on TV and checking the morning newspapers. You want to know what's going on in the world.

Most of your day is spent in meetings with other people. You have visits from some of the people from back home. You attend meetings with other representatives, helping to form new laws. You listen to arguments for and against new laws. You vote for some of the laws and against some others.

You spend a lot of time on the phone, getting and giving information. And you spend a lot of time reading and answering letters from the people back home.

Welcome to the Congress! How do you like your job so far?

Running Congress

Congress, you remember, is made up of two houses or parts. There is the House of Representatives, with 435 members. And there is the Senate, with 100 members. Together, the members of these two houses look at more than 20,000 **bills** a year!

A bill is an idea for a law. Each year, only a few hundred bills become laws.

How do the members of Congress decide which of the 20,000 bills to turn into laws? And how do they keep order in each of their houses? This unit and the next will tell you how.

Leaders Move Things Along

The Congress is like a school or business with many people and a big job to do. Someone has to decide who should do what and when. For example, someone has to decide who should study each of those 20,000 bills! These decisions are made by the leaders in Congress.

Vice-President Bush (left) and Speaker of the House O'Neill listen to President Reagan in the House chamber.

United States House of Representatives

Top Leaders in House and Senate

Who is the top leader in the House of Representatives? A person called the **Speaker of the House** is. The Speaker runs meetings in the House chamber. That's the big room where members of the House come to **debate** and vote on bills. *Debate* means argue for or against something.

The Speaker also makes important decisions about who works on each bill. And if anything happens to the President and the Vice-President, the Speaker becomes the President of the United States.

The top leader in the Senate is the **majority leader**. This is a senator from the party that has the most members in the Senate.

Majority and Minority Leaders

Some members of Congress are Democrats. Some are Republicans. Whichever party has more people in either house is called the **majority party** in that house. The party with fewer members is called the **minority party**.

In each house, there is a majority leader and a minority leader. These leaders help keep the work flowing smoothly between the members of their party. They also look out for their party's interests. For example, they try to get members who belong to their party to vote in favor of bills that the party wants.

Coretta Scott King and two union leaders appear at a hearing. They give their opinions on a bill about jobs.

Rules Must Be Followed

Part of the leaders' job is to make sure the rules of the House and the Senate are followed. Each house has its own set of rules. And each house may punish members who do not obey the rules. In fact, if two-thirds of either house thinks that a member has behaved very badly, they may vote to have that person removed from Congress.

Who says the House and the Senate may do these things? It is all written in the Constitution.

Office Workers

Hundreds of office workers help the representatives and the senators get their work done. There are assistants, secretaries, typists, messengers, and others. Besides the people who work for the whole House or Senate, each member of Congress has his or her own office **staff**.

Leaders, rules, and office workers—all help Congress do its job.

UPI/Bettmann Newsphotos

Committees Share the Load

With 20,000 bills to study every year, how can Congress possibly give each bill more than a moment's attention? The answer is by having **committees**.

A committee is a group of people who work together to find out something, to solve a problem, or to get a job done.

Committees Specialize

Most of the work done on bills in the Congress is done by committees. Each house has about 20 committees that **specialize** in certain kinds of laws. For example, both houses of Congress have committees that specialize in laws about **agriculture** (farming), about the armed services (army, navy, etc.), and about small businesses.

The members of these committees become experts about the needs of farmers, the armed services, the owners of small businesses, or whatever their specialty is. They write bills for laws that will help these groups. And they study bills written by others.

Committees Study and Vote

The committees gather information about each bill they are asked to study. The hold **hearings** (meetings) where they listen to the **opinions** of experts and concerned citizens. They debate the good things and the bad things in the bill.

Finally, the committees vote on the bills they have studied. The bills they **pass** are sent on to the House or Senate chambers for further debate and voting. Many of the 20,000 bills that are written each year never get past the committees.

Where the Ideas Come From

Only a senator or a representative can get a bill started in Congress. But they aren't the only ones who come up with the ideas for new laws. Where else do you think ideas come from?

From the President

Many of the ideas for bills that become laws come from the President's **program**. This program is a plan of things the government can do to help solve the nation's problems.

Presidents can't make laws. So they have to ask Congress to pass the laws that will make their programs work.

From Party Leaders

The members of Congress work closely with the leaders of their parties. Together they decide what to put into certain bills. They plan together how to get bills passed by the whole Congress.

From Special-Interest Groups

Farmers, bankers, workers, hikers—all have special interests. There are hundreds of such special-interest groups in the United States. They all want laws that will help meet their needs.

Many of these groups have special workers called **lobbyists**. These lobbyists spend much of their time talking to members of Congress. Sometimes they give the lawmakers ideas for new laws.

From Private Citizens

Members of Congress get many ideas from private citizens who write or visit them. Sometimes a bill is written to help just one person.

UPI/Bettmann Newsphotos

President Reagan prepares to send his ideas about government spending to Congress.

Informed Citizen

Facts First

Choose the right word or words from the Word List to complete each sentence below.

Word List

majority	Speaker
committees	majority leader
rules	program

1. The top leader in the House of Representatives is the __________ of the House.
2. The top leader in the Senate is the Senate's __________ .
3. The party that has the most members in the House or in the Senate is called the __________ party.
4. The Constitution says that each house of Congress may set up its own __________ .
5. Most of the work of writing and studying bills is done by __________ .
6. Many of the ideas for bills that become laws come from the President's __________ .

Beyond the Facts

Here are some questions to think and talk about.

1. Why do large groups need leaders and rules?
2. A committee will often do a better job than a larger group. Why?
3. Whom do you think members of Congress should listen to most and why?
   a. The President c. Lobbyists
   b. Party leaders d. People back home

Close to Home

Here is something you might like to do.

Find out who your representative and senators are.

Decide on something you would like to tell these people, or on something you would like to find out.

Form a few committees. Have each committee write a letter to a different representative or senator. Here is how you should address your letters:

For Senators

Senator __________
Senator's Name
Senate Office Building
Washington, DC 20510

For Representatives

The Honorable __________
Representative's Name
House Office Building
Washington, DC 20515

unit 9

How Do Bills Become Laws?

Picture this . . .

You are in your home in Washington, D.C., ready to start another day in Congress. You are watching the news on TV. It shows that, in city after city, people are on the march. They want clean air and water. They want an end to **pollution**.

The people carry signs. They sing songs. They listen to speakers.

A few days later, the mail starts pouring in from the people you represent. The letter writers want laws that will help the country stop pollution.

What are you and the others in Congress going to do?

You're going to start writing some bills about pollution, right?

That's what happened back in the early 1970s. Many of the clean-air laws and anti-pollution laws we have now were written and passed then.

The Story of Your Bill

A bill is not a law. It is just a written plan for a law. A lot has to happen before that bill is passed.

Let's follow the steps that a bill has to go through to become a law. In fact, let's make it a bill that you, a member of the House of Representatives, want the Congress to pass.

Let's say that your bill calls for a law that will provide a certain amount of money to help schools teach about protecting the **environment**. *Environment* means the air around us, the woods, the rivers and lakes, and the animals that live in those places.

You Write Your Bill

First, you get all the information you can about what is happening to our environment, and about how schools might teach about the environment. Then you use this information to write a bill.

You Introduce Your Bill

You bring your bill to the desk of the Clerk of the House. That's where all House bills start out.

The Clerk of the House gives your bill a number. For example, the number might be **HR 9432**. (The **H**R stands for **H**ouse of **R**epresentatives.)

The Clerk gets your bill printed and sends copies to the Speaker of the House.

The Speaker Assigns Your Bill

The Speaker decides which committee your bill should go to for study. Since your bill is about helping schools, the Speaker sends it to the Education and Labor Committee.

A Subcommittee Studies Your Bill

The chairperson of the Education and Labor Committee gives your bill to a **subcommittee** called the House Subcommittee on Education. The subcommittee holds special hearings on the bill. It hears the opinions of teachers, students, scientists, artists, business people, and others.

Most of the people at the hearings are in favor of the bill. Some of them suggest a few changes. The members of the subcommittee write in the changes. Then they send your bill back to the chairperson of the Education and Labor Committee. They say that they think the bill should be passed.

The Committee Votes

The chairperson has the committee read your bill with the changes suggested by the subcommittee. The committee votes in favor of your bill.

A Time Is Chosen for House Vote

Once a committee approves a bill, it is usually sent to the Rules Committee. The Rules Committee then picks a time for the bill to be voted on by the House of Representatives. It also makes rules about how much debate will be allowed on the bill before the vote is taken.

However, on the first and third Mondays of every month, bills can go straight to the House. They don't have to go to the Rules Committee first. But these bills must get more votes than usual to pass.

You're sure of the votes; so you ask the committee to send your bill right to the House for voting.

This is where Congress meets—the Capitol building in Washington, D.C. The House and Senate chambers and committee rooms are inside the building.

UPI/Bettmann Newsphotos

The House Debates and Votes

The time comes for the House to debate and vote on your bill. But there is very little debate, because most of the members are for it. The Speaker calls for a vote. The votes are counted.

Those in favor—289.

Those against—28.

Your bill has passed the House easily. But now it has to pass the Senate.

The Senate Passes Your Bill

Your bill goes through almost the same steps in the Senate. It starts with the Secretary of the Senate, who gives it a number that starts with an S (for Senate). Then it goes to a Senate leader who assigns it to a committee.

The committee studies the bill. Committee members make a few changes. Then they vote to approve the bill.

Since there is no Rules Committee in the Senate, the committee sends the bill to the majority leader of the Senate. The majority leader then calls for debate and a vote.

The Senate passes your bill 64-0.

House and Senate Make One Bill

Some members of the House and the Senate form a committee to agree on one final bill. They then send the final bill back to both houses for another vote.

Once again, your bill passes both houses. Now it's ready to go to the President of the United States.

The President Approves

The President reads your bill. He is concerned because the bill calls for spending more than he thinks should be spent. But he knows that most people in the United States would favor the bill. And he knows that it has won favor in the House and the Senate.

So the President decides to sign the bill. The moment he does, it becomes law.

UPI/Bettmann Newsphotos

President Reagan signs a bill.

President Can Veto Bill

If the President doesn't approve of a bill at all, he can **veto** it. That means he can send the bill back to Congress with a letter telling why he doesn't approve of it.

If Congress still wants the bill to become law, it has to take another vote in each house. But this time, two-thirds of the members have to favor the bill in order for it to pass. Then the bill can become law without going back to the President.

Pocket Veto

Here's something else that can happen. If a President keeps a bill for ten days without signing it, the bill automatically becomes law. But if Congress ends its work for the year before the ten days are up, the bill is automatically vetoed. This is called a **pocket veto**.

Based on a True Story

Back in 1970, Congress really did pass a law to help schools teach about the environment. The story of how it was passed is very similar to the story about your bill. We used the story to help you understand how bills become laws.

Informed Citizen

Facts First

Choose the best word or words to complete each sentence below.

1. A bill can be introduced in Congress only by
   a. the President.
   b. a member of Congress.
   c. a citizen.
2. House bills are assigned to committees by
   a. the Speaker of the House.
   b. the Vice-President.
   c. a clerk.
3. Committees often hold
   a. contests.
   b. hearings.
   c. trials.
4. Before a bill goes to the President, it has to pass in
   a. the Senate only.
   b. both the Senate and the House.
   c. the White House.
5. If a President doesn't like a bill, he or she can
   a. change it.
   b. tear it up.
   c. veto it (send it back to Congress).
6. If a President vetoes a bill, it may still become a law if Congress
   a. passes the bill by a two-thirds majority.
   b. holds the bill for ten days.
   c. sends it back to the President.

Beyond the Facts

Here are some questions to think and talk about.

1. It is not easy to get a law passed in Congress. Do you think this is good or bad for the country? Why?
2. What might happen if it were easy to get new laws passed?
3. Do you think the President should have the right to veto bills that a majority of Congress wants? Why or why not?

Close to Home

Here is something you might like to do.

Write bills for class or club rules.

First, form a few committees to study problems that your class or club faces. For example, you might have a Committee on Clean Up.

Choose a chairperson to run the meetings of each committee, and to make reports to the whole group.

Each committee writes a bill for a rule that will help solve a class or club problem. For example: The club will spend $20 to repaint the club room.

A Rules Committee can set up rules for debate and pick a time for voting.

unit 10

What Does the President Do?

Picture this...

After many years in Congress, you ran for President and won. Now you are the President of the United States of America. You were **sworn** into office just a few weeks ago.

At this very moment, you are on your way to the House chamber. You are about to face Congress for the first time as President. You are going there to give a speech to the members of both houses.

This is your first chance to report to the lawmakers. You want to lay out your whole program for them. So you and your staff worked hard on your speech to make it just right.

The door to the House chamber opens as you reach it. Someone announces in a loud voice: "The President of the United States!"

Everyone in the room stands and turns to look at you. You walk to the platform. Millions of people are watching on TV. The world waits to hear your message. What will you tell them?

In 1985, President Chun Doo Hwan of South Korea visited President Reagan. What do you suppose they talked about?

AP/Wide World Photos

Three Jobs in One

Giving speeches is just one of the many things the President has to do. He really has three big jobs rolled into one. Let's see what each of these jobs is about.

Chief Executive

As **chief executive**, the President has to see that federal laws are carried out and enforced. He has to prepare a program to solve the nation's problems. And he has to prepare a **budget** to control government spending. A budget is a plan for spending money.

Chief of State

As chief of state, the President is in charge of our **relations** with other nations. He sees that we have agreements with other nations so that Americans can travel and do business there.

The President also sees that we have treaties with other nations. Treaties are agreements between nations in which they promise to help each other and not to attack each other.

Commander in Chief

About two million men and women serve in the armed forces of the United States. Their commander in chief is—you guessed it—the President.

The President can order the armed forces into action if we are attacked, or if he thinks American lives or interests are in danger overseas. He can also call out the troops anywhere in the United States to put down trouble or to help people in **emergencies**.

U.S. Navy Photograph

The top deck of the Russian ship is loaded with missiles. A U.S. Navy ship has come alongside.

One President's Power in Action

The two strongest nations in the world are the United States and Russia. The governments of the two nations often disagree about many things. But because they respect each other's strength, they have not tried to settle their differences by war.

Still, the people of the world become uneasy whenever the United States and Russia have strong disagreements. They know that both nations have enough power to destroy life on earth.

This was as true back in 1962 as it is today. At that time, John F. Kennedy was President of the United States. And Chairman Nikita Khrushchev was the leader of Russia.

Missiles in Cuba

The Russians had set up some of their **missiles** in Cuba, an island just 90 miles from Florida. Missiles are rocket bombs that can hit cities far away. The Russian missiles were pointed straight at the United States.

President Kennedy told Chairman Khrushchev to take the missiles out of Cuba. Khrushchev said "Nyet!"—which is Russian for "No!" Instead, the Russian leader sent out ships carrying more **weapons** for Cuba.

President Kennedy's Move

President Kennedy knew the next move was up to him. And if he made the wrong move, he might start a war that could destroy the world.

What was he to do? He did not want to let the Russians place more weapons in Cuba, so close to the United States. He wanted to stop them. But if he used too much force, the Russians might feel they had to fight. If he used too little force, the Russians might just laugh at him and go on doing as they pleased.

President Kennedy decided to take a chance. Acting as commander in chief, he sent some U.S. Navy ships into the waters around Cuba. He told the Russians that if their ships tried to pass through, they would be fired upon.

UPI/Bettmann Newsphotos

Chairman Khrushchev and President Kennedy had a friendly meeting in 1961.

Chairman Khrushchev's Move

Now it was the Russian leader's turn to make a move. People all around the world waited to hear what Chairman Khrushchev would do. Would he order the Russian ships to sail on or turn back?

Finally, word came. Chairman Khrushchev ordered the Russian ships to turn around and head for home. No one fired a shot. Soon, the Russians began to remove their missiles from Cuba.

President Kennedy could have done nothing. Or he could have ordered planes to bomb the Russian ships and missiles—an act that might easily have led to war. Instead, he chose to show the power he was ready to use if he had to. This gave the Russians a chance to back away from a fight they really didn't want.

What would you have done if you were in President Kennedy's place?

Replacing a President

What happens if a President dies? Leaves office? Is too sick to work?

- In 1963, just before Thanksgiving, President John F. Kennedy was shot to death. A few hours later, Vice-President Lyndon Johnson was sworn in as President.
- In August of 1974, President Richard Nixon gave up his job. He and some of his closest helpers were charged with trying to cover up their part in a break-in at Democratic party headquarters in Washington, D.C. Many people felt that President Nixon should no longer lead the nation.

  The President knew that he had lost the support of the people. He decided to quit, and Vice-President Gerald Ford became President.
- In March 1981, a man waiting in a crowd shot President Ronald Reagan. The bullet hit the President in the chest, not far from his heart. Would he live or die? If he lived, would he be able to carry on as President?

  The nation waited to see if Vice-President George Bush would have to step into the President's job. But President Reagan lived and soon went back to work.

When a President dies or can't hold office any longer, the Vice-President takes over to keep the nation running. The rule for this comes from Article 2 of the Constitution.

But what happens if the Vice-President also dies or can't serve? Who is next in line to take over?

Right, the Speaker of the House.

UPI/Bettmann Newsphotos

President Kennedy's casket is taken to the cemetery. Who replaced him as President?

Informed Citizen

Facts First

Choose the right word or words from the Word List to complete each sentence below.

Word List

armed forces	enforcing
missiles	ships
treaties	Vice-President

Speaker of the House

1. As chief executive, the President is in charge of carrying out and ________________ the federal laws.
2. As chief of state, the President sees to it that we have agreements and ________________ with other nations.
3. As commander in chief, the President is in charge of the nation's ________________ .
4. President Kennedy wanted Russia to remove its ________________ from Cuba.
5. President Kennedy ordered U.S. Navy ________________ into the waters off Cuba.
6. If a President dies or leaves office, the job is taken over by the ________________ .
7. If that person also dies or can't serve, the President's job goes next to the ________________ .

Beyond the Facts

Here are some questions to think and talk about.

1. A lot of people would like to be President. Why do you think that's so? Would you?
2. Presidents seem to grow older very fast while they are in office. After four years in office, they sometimes look ten years older. Why do you think that happens?
3. What do you think it takes to be a good President?

Close to Home

Here is something you might like to do.

Watch newspapers and magazines for stories about the President. Cut them out. Put them in your scrapbook. Next to each story, write which of the President's three jobs the story is about—chief executive, chief of state, or commander in chief.

Also watch for stories about the President on TV. Talk to classmates, family, and friends about these stories. Maybe they saw the same ones. Discuss which of his jobs the President was doing in each story.

unit 11

Who Works for the President?

Picture this . . .

Your day as President begins early this morning. You start by reading some reports.

The reports are about spring floods washing through five states. One report says that thousands of people have lost their homes. Other reports deal with food shortages, washed-out roads, and power failures.

At 8 a.m. you meet with your advisors. You ask them, "How many shelters are on hand? How much food and medicine is ready to go?"

Your advisors tell you all they can. But they can't tell you what to do. You alone have to decide.

You order troops at nearby army and air force bases to help save lives and property. You order the shipment of food, clothing, medicine, and other supplies.

Soon, thousands of federal troops and workers are carrying out your orders.

Millions of Troops and Workers

Close to two million people in the armed forces and three million government workers help the President carry out his work. But, of course, only a small number of these people work closely with the President.

The White House in Washington, D.C.

UPI/Bettmann Newsphotos

White House Staff

The people who see and work with the President on a day-to-day basis are the members of the White House staff. These are special assistants, speech writers, secretaries, messengers, and others. Most of them work right in the White House, where the President lives and works.

Special Executive Groups

There are also groups of people who work closely with the President on certain kinds of problems. One of these groups is the **O**ffice of **M**anagement and **B**udget (**OMB**). This group helps the President plan the federal government's budget.

Another important group is the National Security Council. This group helps the President find the best way to protect the United States.

Departments and Agencies

Most of the President's millions of helpers work for federal departments and **agencies**. There are about a dozen departments and 1200 agencies.

The difference between a department and an agency is this: A department may be involved with many kinds of problems; agencies usually specialize. For example, an agency called the **I**nternal **R**evenue **S**ervice (**IRS**) collects taxes. And the **F**ederal **B**ureau of **I**nvestigation (**FBI**) gathers information about people who break federal laws.

Executive Departments

The list below names the 13 departments that help the chief executive. Some of these departments were started by our first President, George Washington. Others were added by later Presidents.

As you read over the list, ask yourself, "Does this department serve me in some way? If so, how?"

Department	What It Does
Agriculture	Helps farmers get fair prices and lends them money Teaches new ways to farm Inspects farm plants and animals for disease Manages national forests Manages food stamps
Commerce	Helps American business to grow and run smoothly Helps Americans do business with other countries Gathers important information about the population and the economy Sets standards for weights and measurements Gathers and reports information about the weather
Defense	Runs the armed forces Advises the President on military matters Plans for the nation's defense
Education	Gives money to public schools and colleges Sets up vocational training programs Sets up education programs for the handicapped Collects information about education and teaching Gives money for education research
Energy	Develops national energy plans and programs Works for energy conservation Carries on research into new kinds of energy Makes rules about the sale of electricity and natural gas between states

Department	What It Does
Health and Human Services	Makes sure foods and medicines are safe Gives money for research in health Helps people who are blind or disabled Runs the Social Security program Helps poor people pay for medical care
Housing and Urban Development	Helps rebuild old parts of towns and cities Helps cities clean up pollution Gives loans to build houses and businesses Helps poor people get housing
Interior	Runs the national parks Protects fish and wildlife Manages lands with minerals and forests Helps Native Americans Brings water to dry lands
Justice	Runs the FBI Runs federal prisons Goes to court for the government Takes care of immigration Enforces federal laws
Labor	Gathers job information and sets up training programs Pays unemployment benefits Sets up work safety rules Helps end labor strikes
State	Arranges treaties and agreements Gives out passports Advises the President on our relations with other countries Helps Americans travel and do business in other countries

Department	What It Does
Transportation	Builds federal highways Helps states build highways Makes rules for highway safety Helps railroads and public transportation lines Controls ship and airplane traffic Runs the Coast Guard during peace time
Treasury	Runs the IRS and pays the government's bills Prints and coins money Runs the Secret Service, which guards the President Enforces laws about firearms, tobacco, alcohol, and narcotics (hard drugs)

The Department Heads Form the Cabinet

The heads of these departments are **appointed** by the President, with the Senate's approval. Their titles are **Secretary** of Agriculture, Secretary of Commerce, Secretary of Defense, and so on.

The President often calls on these department heads for their advice on important matters. Sometimes he meets with just one or two at a time. Sometimes he meets with all of them.

This group of department heads is sometimes called the President's **cabinet**.

President Reagan meets with his cabinet.

UPI/Bettmann Newsphotos

Informed Citizen

Facts First

On the left are nine jobs. On the right are the groups that do those jobs. Match each job with the group that does it.

1. Writes speeches for the President	a. Office of Management and Budget (OMB)
2. Plans the federal budget	b. National Security Council
3. Helps protect the United States	c. White House staff
4. Collects taxes	d. Secret Service
5. Gathers information about people who break federal laws	e. Internal Revenue Service (IRS)
6. Guards the President	f. Federal Bureau of Investigation (FBI)
7. Helps farmers	g. Department of Housing and Urban Development
8. Helps cities	h. Department of Labor
9. Helps workers	i. Department of Agriculture

Beyond the Facts

Here are some questions to think and talk about.

1. Which of the agencies and the departments affect your life in some way? How do they affect your life?
2. If you could work for any of the departments or agencies, which would you choose? Why?
3. Why do you think the President needs to have many advisors?

Close to Home

Here is something you might like to do.

Find out if there are any offices of federal departments and agencies in your town, or city. To find out, look in the telephone book under:

UNITED STATES
GOVERNMENT OFFICES

See if you can find any of the departments or agencies you have read about in this unit. Call or write one of them. Ask someone to visit your class to tell you about his or her work.

unit 12

Who Pays for Government?

Picture this...

You are still the President of the United States. And you are sitting in your White House office, trying to work out some budget problems.

Here are some of the things you have to plan on paying for.

- Salaries for troops and government workers
- Ships, planes, and weapons
- Aid to the poor, the sick, and the jobless
- Aid to victims of floods and other disasters
- Building and repairing federal highways

This list is just a start. You're going to need more than $900 *billion* to pay all the bills. That's enough to buy a good motorcycle for every man, woman, and child in the United States!

Where are you going to get the money?

From the taxpayers, of course.

Income Taxes

Perhaps you or someone you know is a taxpayer. If you earn above a certain amount of money in any given year, you have to pay part of that money to the government. The part you pay is called an **income** tax.

Most of the federal government's **revenue** comes from income taxes. *Revenue* is money that the government collects in different ways.

IRS Collects

Congress decides how much tax money is needed each year, but the Internal Revenue Service (IRS) collects the money. How? By telling your employer to **deduct**, or take out, a certain amount of money from your pay every payday. Your employer must then send that money to the government.

At the end of the year, your employer must tell you how much you earned during the year and how much was deducted for income tax.

You Report

Then you have to fill out an income tax form. On this form you report how much you earned. You may list certain expenses. Then you figure out how much tax you owe for the year.

If your employer has deducted enough to cover what you owe, you won't have to pay any more income tax. If the deductions don't cover what you owe, you will have to pay the difference. If more was deducted than what you owe, you will get some money back from the government.

Every year, millions of Americans have to fill out an income tax form like this one.

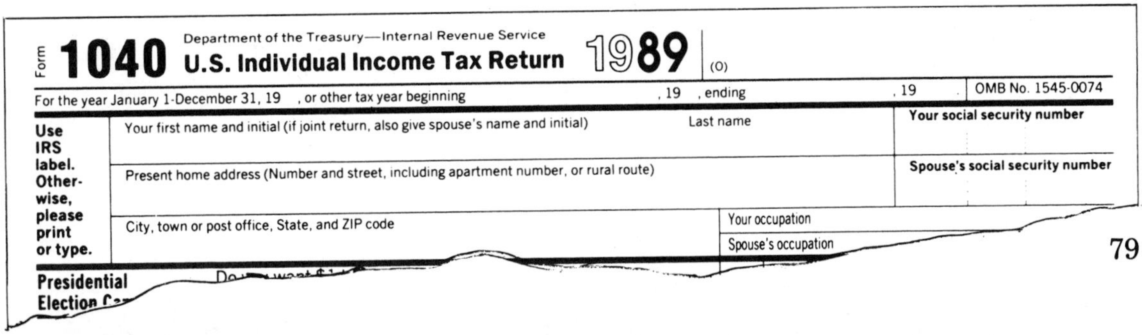
Form 1040 Department of the Treasury—Internal Revenue Service
U.S. Individual Income Tax Return 1989 (0)
For the year January 1-December 31, 19 , or other tax year beginning , 19 , ending , 19 OMB No. 1545-0074
Use IRS label. Other-wise, please print or type.
Your first name and initial (if joint return, also give spouse's name and initial) Last name Your social security number
Present home address (Number and street, including apartment number, or rural route) Spouse's social security number
City, town or post office, State, and ZIP code Your occupation Spouse's occupation
Presidential Election

Excise and Sales Taxes

You also pay taxes on many goods and services you buy. The amount charged for these taxes is anywhere from 2 to 12 cents on every dollar you spend.

Such taxes are called **excise** and sales taxes. *Excise* usually refers to taxes the federal government charges on goods and services. *Sales taxes* usually refers to taxes charged by state and local governments.

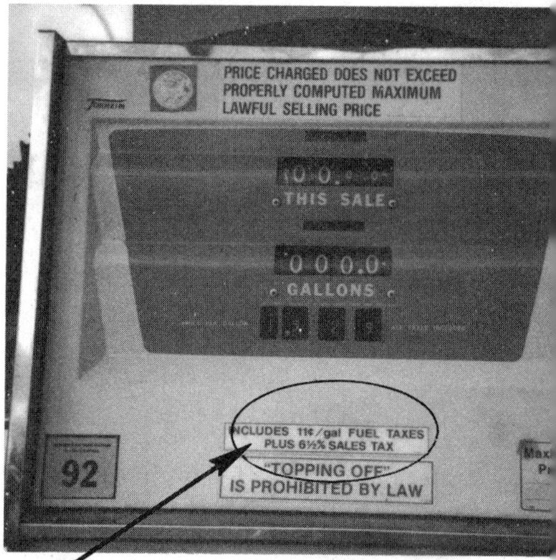

Federal, state, and local taxes are included in the price of gas.

Excise Taxes

You have to pay federal excise taxes on many goods and services that the government thinks you don't absolutely need in order to live. For example, you pay an excise tax if you buy gas or cigarettes and when you make a telephone call.

Sales Taxes

Many of the same things that are taxed by the federal government are also taxed by some state and local governments. But the state or local tax on these things is called a sales tax. State or local governments that have sales taxes may tax almost everything you buy. Most governments, however, do not tax food or medicine.

Stores and other businesses may include excise and sales taxes in the prices marked on things they sell. But usually they add the taxes to the prices later—when you pay for the things you buy. The stores and businesses send the tax money they collect to the local, state, and federal governments.

If you buy things this week, see if you can find out how much you are paying for excise or sales taxes.

Other Government Revenues

Besides the taxes you have learned about so far, governments have other ways to get the revenues they need. Here are some of those ways.

Did you ever pay a fine for parking where a sign told you not to?

Social Security Tax

When people are old enough to retire from work, they may be able to collect Social Security benefits. The money to pay for this comes from the Social Security tax that is deducted from people's pay.

Import Taxes

The federal government charges **duties** or **import** taxes on goods that come here from other countries. For example, if you buy a camera that was made in another country, the price may include the amount charged for an import tax.

Fines and Licenses

All three levels of government collect fines from people who break laws. Industries pay federal fines for breaking safety and pollution laws. Drivers pay local fines for parking in no-parking areas.

Each level of government also sells licenses and permits. TV and radio stations get licenses from the federal government. Drivers, hunters, and doctors get licenses from their state governments. And businesses get permits from their local governments.

Property Taxes

State and local governments also get money from property taxes. These are taxes charged to the owners of land and buildings. Local governments get most of their money this way.

Who Decides How Much?

The Constitution says that Congress "shall have the power to lay and collect taxes, duties,... and excises."

Congress and the President

All bills about federal taxes start in the House of Representatives. Then they go through all the steps you read about in unit 9 before they become laws.

But it is really the President who leads the way in deciding how much tax revenue will be needed. Once the President knows what he wants to do and how much everything will cost, he tries to get Congress to raise the amount of money needed.

The lawmakers don't always go along with what the President wants. Then they and the President have to work out their differences until they reach some agreement.

Congress May Borrow Money

If Congress can't raise enough tax money to pay all the bills, it may borrow money. But just like you and me, Congress has to pay **interest** when it borrows. Interest is the amount of extra money you have to pay back when you get a loan from a bank.

In recent years, the federal government has had to borrow a lot of money, and pay a lot of interest. Tax revenues have just not been enough to pay all the bills.

Of course, Congress could just raise everyone's taxes much higher than they've been. Why do you suppose the lawmakers haven't done this?

Right. Taxpayers might get really upset. Then they might not vote for those lawmakers when election time comes again.

Informed Citizen

Facts First

Decide if each statement below is true or false. If you think it is false, be ready to tell why you think so.

True or False

1. The government gets most of the money it needs from taxes the American people pay.
2. The Constitution gave the President the power to collect taxes.
3. Congress may borrow money.
4. The more money you earn, the less income tax you have to pay.
5. The job of collecting income taxes belongs to the courts.
6. Money for income taxes is deducted from people's paychecks.
7. Excise and sales taxes are taken out of people's paychecks too.
8. Charging property taxes on land and buildings is the main way local governments get their revenues.

Beyond the Facts

Here are some questions to think and talk about.

1. What kinds of taxes have you had to pay?
2. How do you feel about having to pay taxes?
3. People always complain about taxes. But we can't seem to do without them. Why do you think this is so?

Close to Home

Here are some things you might like to do.

1. Find out more about your state and local taxes. How much do you have to pay in sales taxes? What are the tolls on bridges and roads near you? How much does your state charge for a driver's license? For car registration?
2. One thing you'll do every time you start a new job is fill in a form for income tax deductions. It's called a Form W-4. Ask your teacher to get a copy and show you how to fill it in. You might also want to learn how to fill in a Form 1040. That's the form on which you report your earnings and deductions to the IRS.

unit 13

What Do the Courts Do?

Picture this...

Tiny and Marie are returning from South America. They pick up their baggage and go through **customs**.

The customs **inspector** takes a quick look through Tiny's bag and tells him he can leave. But then he suddenly says to Tiny, "Wait a minute! Let me see your cap."

"My cap?" Tiny asks. "What for?"

"Just hand it over," says the inspector.

The inspector feels the inside and outside of the cap. He takes a small knife and slits the lining. Out fall several small bags of fine, white powder.

"How did they get in there?" Tiny asks with alarm.

"You must have picked up someone else's cap," says Marie.

"You both better come with me," says the inspector.

Later, Tiny and Marie are arrested for bringing **illegal** drugs into the country.

Criminal Cases

Are Tiny and Marie guilty or not guilty? That's for a court to decide. But they have been accused of committing a crime; so they will get a **criminal** trial.

A criminal trial is the kind you often see in movies or on TV. These trials usually take place in a criminal court, before a judge and a jury. However, a **defendant** may choose to have his or her case heard by a judge alone. A defendant is a person who is on trial.

Members of a jury are picked from the community.

The Jury's Job

There are usually 12 people on a jury. What do you think their job is?

The jury's job is to decide if the defendant is guilty or not guilty. The judge asks the jury to listen carefully to all the **evidence**, or facts, in the case. And he or she explains things the jury needs to know in order to make its decision.

The Verdict

At the end of the trial, the members of the jury go into another room and talk about the case. They try to decide if the defendant is guilty or not guilty. Their decision is called a **verdict**.

The jury returns to the courtroom and gives its verdict. If the verdict is "guilty," the judge decides what the defendant's punishment will be. If the verdict is "not guilty," the defendant goes free. If the members of the jury aren't able to agree on a verdict, the defendant may get another trial or may be set free.

Picture this...

Carol Ramos is a waitress. She bought a new car several months ago, with money she had saved from her tips.

Last month she was in a bad accident. The other driver was from another state and had no car insurance. The accident was his fault.

Carol is angry. Repairs on her car cost close to $1,000. In addition, she was hurt in the accident. She has another $1,000 in medical bills. Besides that, she couldn't work for several weeks. So she has lost the money she could have earned in tips.

Carol has asked the other driver to pay her bills and to make up for the money she has lost at work. The other driver refuses to pay a penny. What can Carol do?

Civil Cases

Carol can **sue** the other driver. That means she can take the other driver to court, and ask the court to order the other driver to pay her.

If Carol wins the case, the other driver may have to pay all her costs from the accident. He may also have to pay her lawyer's **fees** and court fees, plus something to make up for her lost income.

This kind of case is called a **civil** case and is tried in a civil court. Civil cases do not involve crimes like theft, robbery, or murder. They involve things like money, property, accidents, and **contracts**. A contract is an agreement to do business.

If only a small amount of money is involved, the case may be handled in a **small claims court**. Such courts usually handle cases that involve less than $1,500. The amount may be different in your state.

Courtesy Santa Clara County

Local courts like this one are part of the state court system.

Federal and State Courts

Both the federal government and the state governments have courts. If a person is accused of breaking a federal law, he or she will be tried in a federal court.

For example, Tiny and Marie are accused of bringing illegal drugs into the country. That is against federal law. So Tiny and Marie will be tried in a federal criminal court.

If a case involves people from two or more states, it will also be tried in a federal court. For example, Carol is suing a driver from another state. So her case will be tried in a federal civil court.

Here are some other kinds of cases that would be tried in a federal court. A case is also tried in federal court if it involves

- the United States government or any of its **officials**;
- members of the governments of other nations;
- the governments of two or more states;
- the government of a state and the government of another nation;
- a citizen of the United States and the government of another nation; or
- a citizen of the United States and a citizen of another nation.

All other cases are handled by state courts.

Suppose someone lives in Ashland, Oregon. And suppose that person wants to sue a plumber in Ashland for doing bad work in her house. Would the case go to a federal court or a state court?

Right. It would go to a state court.
Would it go to a criminal court or a civil court?

Right. It would go to a civil court.

Picture this...

The jury in Tiny and Marie's trial decides they are guilty. But Tiny and Marie still say they are not guilty. And their lawyer believes them.

What can Tiny and Marie do?

They can ask their lawyer to **appeal** the jury's verdict. That is, they can ask the judges of a higher court, a court of appeals, to review their case.

Courts of Appeals

Courts in the United States are arranged in a system of low, middle, and high courts. Traffic courts are on the low end. Trial courts, like the one where Tiny and Marie's case was heard, are in the middle. And courts of appeals are on the high end.

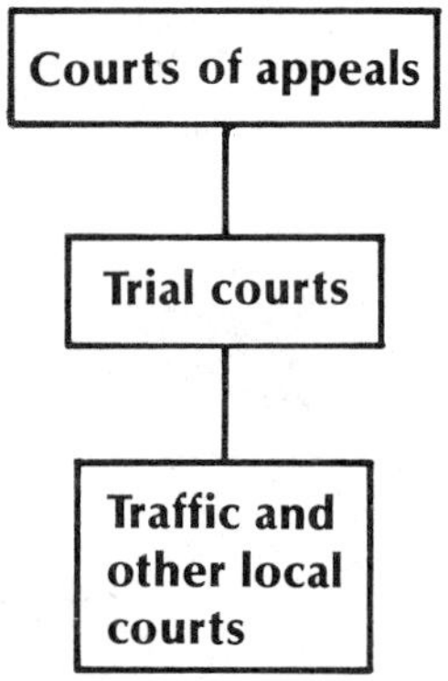

What all that means is this: A decision made in a trial court is not always final. A higher court may disagree with that decision. If it does, the higher court can **reverse**, or change, the verdict of the lower court.

Here's how a court of appeals works.

The judges from the court of appeals decide whether or not there seems to be a good reason for the appeal. If there does, the judges read a full report of the trial. They may also listen to the lawyers from both sides of the case.

Finally, the judges make a decision. They may decide to agree with the verdict of the trial court. Or they may reverse the decision of the trial court.

Let's look back at Tiny and Marie's case. If a court of appeals reverses the verdict of the trial court, Tiny and Marie may go free. Or they may be held for retrial.

Informed Citizen

Facts First

Choose the right word from the Word List to complete each sentence below.

Word List

appeal	criminal
civil	state
reverse	verdict

1. People who are accused of committing crimes are tried in ______________ courts.
2. Trials in which one person sues another person are held in ______________ courts.
3. If a jury cannot agree on a ______________, the defendant may get another trial or may go free.
4. If a defendant feels that he or she did not get a fair trial, he or she may ______________ to a higher court.
5. Higher courts may ______________ the verdicts of lower courts.
6. Both the federal government and the ______________ governments have courts.

Beyond the Facts

Here are some questions to think and talk about.

1. Would you like to serve on a jury? Why or why not?
2. If you were on trial, would you want your case to be heard and decided by a jury or by a judge alone? Why?
3. What do you think might be some good reasons for appealing a case to a higher court?

Close to Home

Here are some things you might like to do.

1. Check local newspapers and TV news shows for stories about trials. Cut out the stories you find in newspapers and paste them in your scrapbook. Discuss the stories with classmates, family, and friends. Or pretend to be a TV news reporter and present the news to your class.
2. Find out what kinds of courts there are in your town, city, or area. Are there any federal courts? State courts? Do they have both criminal and civil trials? Is there a small claims court?
3. Visit one of the courts and see what you can learn about what the court does and how it works.

Why Is the Supreme Court Special?

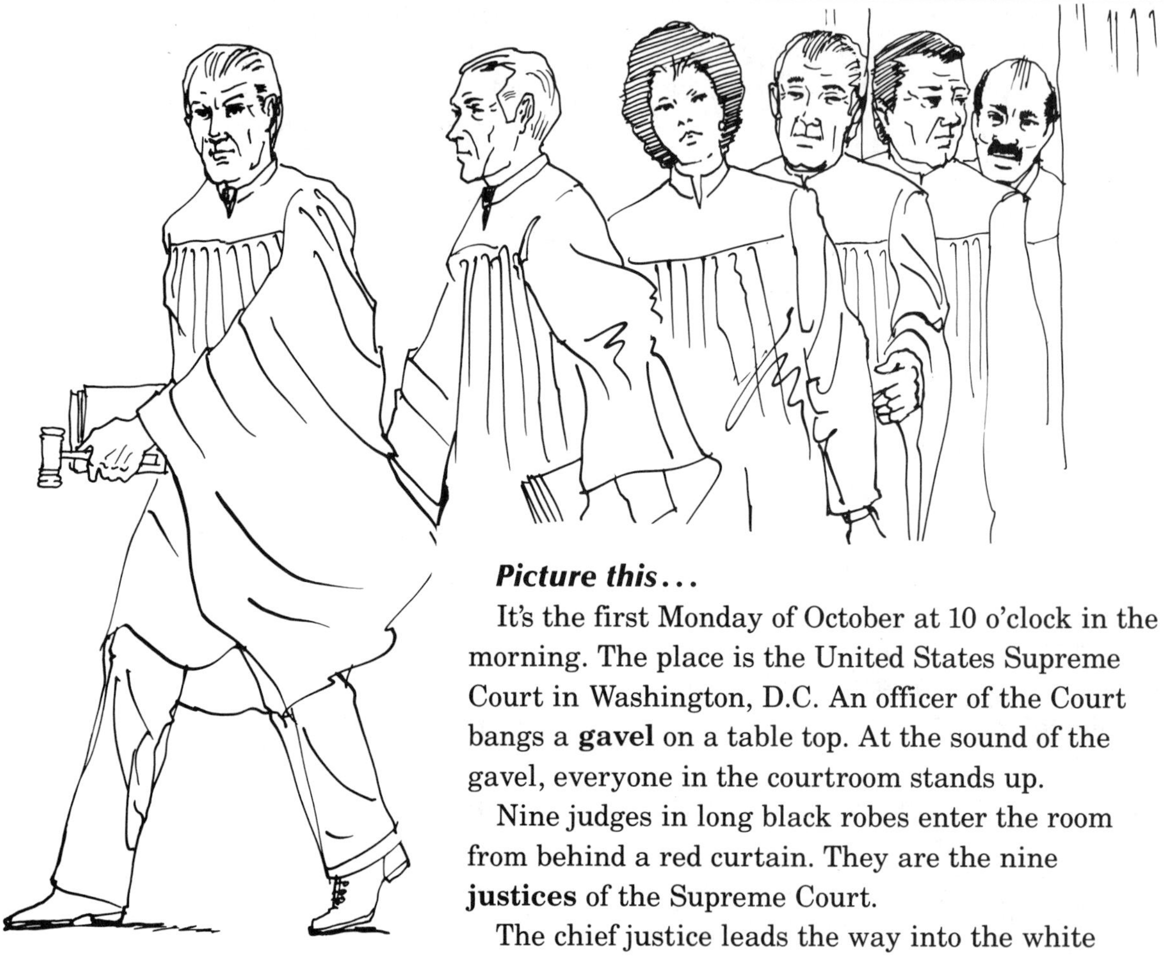

Picture this . . .

It's the first Monday of October at 10 o'clock in the morning. The place is the United States Supreme Court in Washington, D.C. An officer of the Court bangs a **gavel** on a table top. At the sound of the gavel, everyone in the courtroom stands up.

Nine judges in long black robes enter the room from behind a red curtain. They are the nine **justices** of the Supreme Court.

The chief justice leads the way into the white marble courtroom. He walks to the tallest chair in the middle of nine black chairs at the high bench. The other justices take their places.

The officer of the Court calls, "Oyez! Oyez! Oyez!" These old words mean "Give me your attention!" The words are used to signal the start of the day's work.

The justices take their seats. Then everyone else sits. The Supreme Court is about to hear some appeals.

The Highest Court of Appeals

The Supreme Court is the highest court of appeals in the nation. No other court can reverse its decisions. In other words, it has the final say on any case of law.

Justices Pick Cases

Every year, thousands of people appeal their cases to the Supreme Court. But the nine justices can't deal with more than a few hundred cases a year. So they pick the ones that seem most important.

The justices listen to the lawyers from both sides of each case they agree to hear. And they study all the trial reports from those cases. They also see what their law books have to say about cases similar to the ones they are studying.

Then the justices meet together behind the locked doors of a guarded room. There they make decisions about the cases they have heard and studied.

Majority Decisions

Decisions are made by majority rule. That is, whatever a majority of the justices agrees on becomes the decision of the Supreme Court. So, all nine justices don't have to agree in order to have a decision. Only five or more must agree.

Every time the Supreme Court makes a decision, a justice who voted with the majority writes a paper to explain the decision. Sometimes, a justice who did not vote with the majority writes a paper to explain why he or she did not agree.

These papers help everyone understand the reasons for the decision. They also help lawyers and judges who may work on similar cases in the future.

UPI/Bettmann Newsphotos

From left to right are Justices Harry Blackmun, Thurgood Marshall, William Brennan, Warren Burger, Sandra Day O'Connor, Byron White, Lewis Powell, William Rehnquist, and John Paul Stevens.

Guardian of the Constitution

Because it is the highest court in the nation, the Supreme Court has a special job to do. It watches over the highest law in the nation—the Constitution.

As **guardian** of the Constitution, the Supreme Court helps make sure that no one takes away our basic rights. And it settles disagreements about what the words in the Constitution mean.

The Supreme Court can also tell members of the government that their actions or laws are unconstitutional. That is, they can say that certain actions or laws go against the Constitution.

The Supreme Court can

- tell a President or other elected leader that a certain action is unconstitutional;
- tell Congress or state and local lawmakers that a certain law is unconstitutional; and
- tell other courts that a certain decision is unconstitutional.

Let's look now at some of the decisions that the Supreme Court has made in recent years.

1954: Separate Schools

Up until 1954, some states had laws that said black children and white children could not go to the same schools. Many black parents thought that the schools for black children did not offer as good an education as the schools for white children did. So the parents wanted their children to be able to go to the same schools as white children went to.

The parents got a lawyer to help them. When the case came before the Supreme Court, the lawyer won.

The Court ruled that the state laws about separate schools were unconstitutional because they went against the Fourteenth Amendment to the Constitution. That amendment says that no state may deny any person "the equal protection of the laws."

UPI/Bettmann Newsphotos

The Supreme Court Building in Washington, D.C.

1962: School Prayers

Up until 1962, most schools began their day with a prayer. Many parents did not approve of this. They said that prayers are part of religion, not education.

These parents said that the children in public schools were of different religions. So they did not think it was fair to make all children say the same prayer.

In 1963, the Supreme Court ruled that schools could not force students to say a prayer. The Court said forcing students to pray was unconstitutional because it denied one of the four freedoms given in the First Amendment—freedom of religion.

1981: The Draft

In certain times of danger to the nation, the Congress may pass a law to **draft** people into the armed forces. This means people have to serve, whether they want to or not.

In the past, only men have been drafted, not women. Some people thought that this was unconstitutional. They said that if men were to be drafted, women should be too.

But when the case came before the Supreme Court, the justices ruled that Congress could pass a law to draft men only. The Court said that Congress has that right because the Constitution gives Congress wide powers in matters of national defense.

Two Justices

The Supreme Court has become an important means for people to win and hold on to their rights in the United States. To do this well, the Court must represent all Americans.

But, for a long time, all of the justices were men. And all of them were white. There were no women. There were no members of minority groups.

First Black Justice

Thurgood Marshall was the first black person to become a Supreme Court justice. Marshall was the lawyer who won the case about separate schools for blacks.

President Kennedy made Marshall a federal judge. Later, President Johnson gave Marshall a job in the Justice Department. Then, when there was an opening on the Supreme Court in 1967, President Johnson appointed Marshall to the Court with the Senate's approval.

UPI/Bettmann Newsphotos

Thurgood Marshall

Sandra Day O'Connor

UPI/Bettmann Newsphotos

First Woman Justice

For a long time, many people have felt there should be women on the Court. In 1981, Sandra Day O'Connor became the first woman Supreme Court justice.

O'Connor had already had a long career in law. She had also been in the Arizona State Senate.

But when the time came for O'Connor to choose between working with laws or making laws, she chose working with laws. Soon she became a judge on the Arizona State Court of Appeals.

In 1981, there was an opening on the Supreme Court. President Reagan knew it was time to name a woman for the job. The woman he named was Sandra Day O'Connor. The Senate soon gave its approval.

Informed Citizen

Facts First

Decide if each statement below is true or false. If you think it is false, be ready to tell why you think so.

True or False

1. Presidents appoint Supreme Court justices to their jobs.
2. The justices study cases, listen to lawyers from both sides, study trial reports and law books, and then make their decisions.
3. The Supreme Court hears all the cases that people bring to it.
4. The Supreme Court is the highest court of appeals, and no other court can reverse its decisions.
5. The Supreme Court is the guardian of the Constitution.
6. The Supreme Court has no power over the President and the Congress.
7. The Supreme Court has done much to help protect people's basic rights.
8. To this day, there has never been a black justice or a woman justice.

Beyond the Facts

Here are some questions to think and talk about.

1. Why do you think the writers of the Constitution gave the Supreme Court the right to check on what the President and the Congress do?
2. The Supreme Court has often played a big role in protecting people's rights. Do you think that's an important role for the Court to play? Why?
3. A black and a woman now serve on the Supreme Court. Why is it important to have justices from different groups on the Court?

Close to Home

Here are some things you might like to do.

1. Watch for news about new Supreme Court decisions on TV and in the newspapers. Some of these decisions might affect your life or the lives of people you know. Discuss the decisions with your classmates, family, and friends.
2. Hold a Supreme Court Day in class. Choose people to play the justices, the lawyers, and the officer of the Court.

Is the Constitution Still Working?

Picture this . . .

The police are about to question Mary Chase about stealing money from her boss.

OFFICER: Mary Chase, you are charged with stealing money. It is our duty to inform you of your rights before we begin to ask questions.

MARY: You mean I've got rights? Even in here?

OFFICER: First, you have the right to remain silent. Anything you say can and will be used against you in a court of law. Second, you have the right to talk to a lawyer and have the lawyer present with you while you are being questioned. Third, if you cannot afford to hire a lawyer, one will be appointed to be with you during any questioning, if you wish to have one present.

MARY: Well, I can't afford a lawyer, but I'd sure like one here when you question me.

OFFICER: OK, Ms. Chase. You will have to wait in a cell until the lawyer gets here.

The Miranda Case

Why did the police have to tell Mary Chase about her rights? Because of a Supreme Court decision made in 1966.

The case before the Supreme Court was about the rights of a man named Ernesto Miranda. The court based its decision on the Fifth and Sixth Amendments to the Constitution. Those are the amendments that tell about the rights of people who are arrested.

Here's what happened.

UPI/Bettmann Newsphotos

Ernesto Miranda

Didn't Know His Rights

Ernesto Miranda was arrested for a crime in Arizona in 1963. At the police station, no one told him about his constitutional rights. He didn't know he could have a lawyer. He didn't know he didn't have to say anything to the police.

Miranda just answered the police officers' questions. And after a few hours, he signed a **confession**.

Later, Miranda was given a lawyer and put on trial. His confession was used against him. He was found guilty and sent to prison.

Appeal Reaches Supreme Court

Miranda's lawyer thought that the confession wasn't fair. After all, Miranda didn't know his rights when he signed it. So the lawyer decided to appeal the verdict. By 1966, the case had made it all the way to the Supreme Court.

The Court agreed with the lawyer. The Court said Americans have the right to be told their constitutional rights if they are arrested. So now, when people are arrested, they must be told about their rights to remain silent and to have a lawyer.

UPI/Bettmann Newsphotos

In 1963, Martin Luther King, Jr., led a civil rights march in Washington, D.C. What do you suppose the marchers hoped to gain by marching in the nation's capital?

Picture this...

Late on the night of December 1, 1955, a black woman boards a city bus. She is going home from work. Her feet hurt, and she is tired. When she sees a seat in the middle of the bus, she takes it.

The bus moves on. At the next stop, more people get on. Then a lot more people get on at the next stop. The bus is crowded. People are standing in the aisle.

The bus driver calls back to the woman, "Get up and give your seat to the white person standing next to you."

The woman seems about to do it. But then she changes her mind. "No," she answers. "I'm not going to move." And she stays put.

The driver calls a police officer. And before Rosa Parks knows it, she's in jail.

Civil Rights

But what law was Rosa Parks accused of breaking? A city law saying blacks could sit only in the back of a bus. It was just one of many **segregation** laws that denied blacks their civil rights.

The segregation laws kept blacks from getting good jobs and living in nice homes. They separated blacks from whites in public places. And many of them made it hard for blacks to vote.

The arrest of Rosa Parks led to a Supreme Court decision that said such laws were unconstitutional. Here's how it all happened.

Bus Boycott

Most of the blacks in Montgomery, Alabama, where Rosa Parks lived, joined together under the leadership of Martin Luther King, Jr. For a year, they **boycotted** the city buses by not riding on them. The city lost a lot of money, but still the law didn't change.

Finally, late in 1956, Rosa Parks's case reached the Supreme Court. The Court ruled that segregation of blacks in public places was unconstitutional under the Fourteenth Amendment. This amendment guarantees all Americans "the equal protection of the laws."

Voters' Rights

The Supreme Court wasn't the only part of the government working to help blacks get their civil rights. Congress also took up the cause and passed many laws to end segregation.

One of those laws was the Voting Rights Act of 1965. It enforces the Fifteenth Amendment, which gives blacks the right to vote. Under the law, federal workers are sent to **register** blacks in places where local laws have kept them from signing up to vote.

The Equal Rights Amendment

There are other Americans besides blacks who feel they don't get all their rights. Among them are many women.

Women won the right to vote in 1920. The Nineteenth Amendment gave it to them. But so far, they haven't won equality with men in many other important ways. That's especially true when it comes to work.

Women now work at many jobs that once were only for men. But women are often paid less than men are paid. And they often don't get the top jobs.

NOW and ERA

A woman's group was formed in the 1960s to see what could be done to help women win equality with men. The group is called the **N**ational **O**rganization for **W**omen (**NOW**).

NOW joined with other women's groups. Together they got Congress to pass the **E**qual **R**ights **A**mendment (**ERA**) in 1972. This amendment says that equal rights under the law can't be denied to women.

Not Approved

To become part of the Constitution, the ERA had to be approved by at least 38 states. That had to happen by June 30, 1982.

When that time came, only 35 states had approved the ERA. So the amendment did not become part of the Constitution.

In 1982, women's groups began working again for an equal rights amendment. The constitution protects their right to do this. Do you think they'll win next time? Why or why not?

The San Francisco Examiner

Women's groups say they will continue to fight for women's rights and for an equal rights amendment.

Informed Citizen

Facts First

Choose the best words to complete each sentence below.

1. Because of the Miranda case, police must now tell an arrested person that he or she has the right to
   a. remain silent and have a lawyer.
   b. sign a confession and go to jail.
   c. appeal the case and go free.
2. Before the Rosa Parks case, blacks in some cities and towns had to
   a. stand in the aisle of a bus.
   b. ride in separate buses.
   c. sit in the back of a bus.
3. Segregation laws kept blacks from
   a. going to school.
   b. riding on buses.
   c. getting good jobs.
4. In Rosa Parks's case, the Supreme Court ruled that segregation was
   a. OK in public places.
   b. unconstitutional.
   c. guaranteed by the Fourteenth Amendment.
5. The purpose of the Equal Rights Amendment is to give
   a. blacks equal rights with whites.
   b. children equal rights with parents.
   c. women equal rights with men.

Beyond the Facts

Here are some things to think and talk about.

1. If you were arrested, what would be some of your rights, based on the Miranda case?
2. What other groups besides blacks and women think they don't have equal rights? Do you agree with them?
3. Do you think the Constitution is still working? Why or why not?

Close to Home

Here are some things you might like to do.

1. Review what you have learned. Form several teams. Have each team read again one or two units of this book. Then have each team tell the class the main ideas in the unit or units it read.
2. After the review, choose up sides for a game of Informed Citizen. Have the teacher or someone else ask questions from the Facts First exercise at the end of each unit. Or make up questions to ask. Make up your own rules for how to play the game and for choosing a winner.

Part 2

From City Hall to State Capitol

Introduction

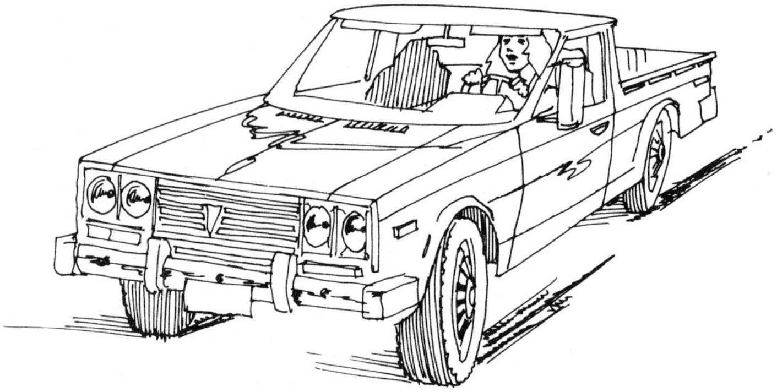

Have you ever had thoughts like these?

"Government seems so far away."
"What does it really have to do with me?"
"What does it do for me?"
"Do I have any say in my local government?"
"How do I find out?"

Local government is all around you. Many services you depend on are provided by local governments. In your city or town, and in your county, it's local government that makes laws to protect you and all the people who live there.

You can call on local government for help when you need it. And you can have a say in how your local government is run, and in who runs it. The same is true for your state government.

Part 2 of *Our Government in Action* will help you get to know your local and state governments better. It will help you understand who does what in each government, and how each government works. It will also help you learn how to take part in choosing the people who make laws and run government.

unit 16

What Are Local Laws About?

Picture this...

Jenny Kurtz is in trouble. She just broke a local law.

Jenny took her dog for a run in the park. The dog was running around without a leash. A jogger came by. The dog got excited and jumped at the jogger.

The jogger got scared. He tried to push the dog away. But the dog got angry and bit him.

Now the jogger's arm is bleeding. He will have to see a doctor. And the dog will have to be tested for an illness called rabies. If the dog has rabies, the jogger will have to get special shots from the doctor. The shots will keep the jogger from getting sick.

What should Jenny have done to keep her dog from biting the jogger?

If you own a dog, you probably already know the answer. Jenny should have kept her dog on a leash.

The San Jose Mercury News

Animal control officers enforce local laws about animals. Why might they be picking up this dog?

Laws About Animals

Most towns and cities have laws about keeping a dog on a leash outdoors. They also have laws that make dog owners buy licenses for their dogs. Other laws say that owners must have their dogs checked for diseases.

Owners must control their dogs. If a dog hurts someone, the law says that the owner of the dog is **responsible**. That means the owner can be fined or made to pay for **damages**.

Protecting People

Many towns and cities have laws against keeping certain kinds of animals as pets. They have laws against keeping a dangerous animal, such as a wildcat or a rattlesnake, as a pet. And they have laws against raising chickens or rabbits in an apartment. These laws are made to keep people from being harmed or annoyed by animals.

Protecting Pets

Most towns and cities also have laws to keep animals from being hurt by people. A dog owner who beats or starves his dog can be arrested or fined.

In most cities, all these laws about animals are enforced by animal control **officers**.

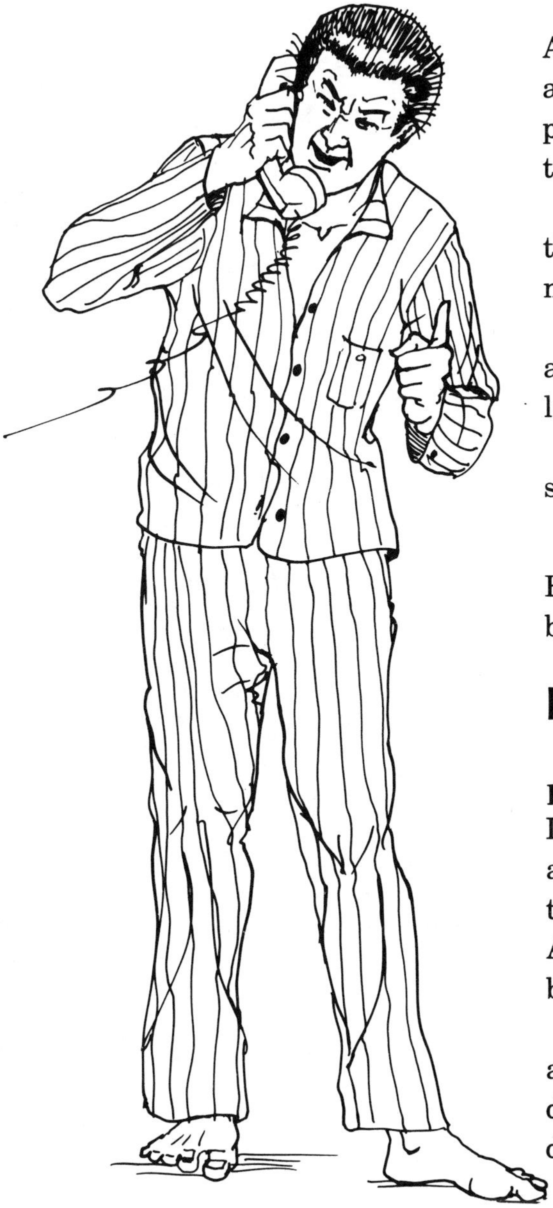

Picture this...

Tony went to bed early because tomorrow is going to be a tough day. He has to be at work by 6 o'clock in the morning.

But it's 1 a.m. now, and Tony is wide awake. A noise woke him. It's coming from the next apartment, where a party is going on. A record player is going full blast. And Tony can't get back to sleep.

Tony is angry. He picks up the phone and calls the people next door. "I can't sleep," he says. "You're making too much noise!"

The person at the other end of the phone laughs and hangs up. Then the music and the noise get louder.

What can Tony do to stop the noise and get some sleep?

If you said, "Call the police," you're right. Why? Because the people having the loud party are breaking the law.

Disturbing the Peace

The people at the party are **disturbing the peace**. That means they are bothering other people. In this case, the noise of the party is keeping Tony and a lot of other people awake. Most of them have to get up in the morning to go to work or to school. And the law says that they have a right not to be bothered.

Most towns and cities also have other laws about making noise or bothering people during the day. Can you think of one way a person might be disturbing the peace even during the day?

How about playing a radio loud in a crowded bus or shouting and fighting in a restaurant? Some cities have laws against doing these things.

Picture this...

It's Friday night. Liz goes to a movie with Ron. When she gets back home, she knows right away that something is wrong. Her apartment door is open. And one of the windows is broken.

"Somebody broke in," Liz says to Ron. "I'm going to call the police."

Liz calls the police and tells them what happened.

"Anything stolen?" a police officer asks.

"I don't think so," Liz says.

"Any damage done?" the officer asks.

"A broken window," Liz answers. "Also some smashed dishes and picture frames."

"OK," the officer says. "We'll check into it."

In this case, nothing was stolen from Liz's home. But somebody broke two local laws. Can you name the two things somebody did that are against the law?

Trespassing and Vandalism

First, somebody broke a law by breaking into Liz's apartment. Breaking into someone's house, apartment, or place of business is called **trespassing**.

Second, somebody smashed Liz's window, dishes, and picture frames. Damaging things that belong to someone else is called **vandalism**.

The laws against these things are made to protect people and their property. *Property* means things someone owns.

Suppose somebody slashes the tires of your car or bicycle. Would that be trespassing or vandalism?

Right. That's vandalism.

Suppose somebody breaks into a grocery store. Would that be trespassing or vandalism?

Right. That's trespassing.

Protecting People and Property

Most local laws are made to protect the people and property in a town or a city. Those laws cover a wide range of things, from spitting on the sidewalk to firing a gun on Main Street. Here are a few more examples:

- Traffic laws tell you where you can drive your car and how fast you can drive it. They tell what **signals** you have to obey and where you can park your car. Most cities also have laws about where you can ride a bicycle, roller-skate, or use a skate board.
- Fire laws tell you whether you can smoke in public places such as movie theaters or department stores.
- Noise laws tell you how loud you can play your radio on a bus or a train.
- Health laws tell you where and how you have to get rid of your garbage.

Informed Citizen

Facts First

Decide if each statement below is true or false. If you think it is false, be ready to tell why you think so.

True or False?

1. Most towns and cities have laws about keeping a dog on a leash outdoors.
2. The owner of a dog is not responsible if his dog bites another person.
3. Many towns and cities have laws against keeping dangerous animals as pets.
4. *Disturbing the peace* means bothering other people.
5. Some cities have laws against playing a radio loud on a bus.
6. Destroying property that doesn't belong to you is called trespassing.
7. Breaking into someone else's house, apartment, or place of business is called vandalism.
8. Laws against trespassing and vandalism are made to protect people and their property.

Beyond the Facts

Here are some questions to think and talk about.

1. What are some local laws that affect your life almost every day?
2. Why do you think your local government made those laws?
3. What laws do you think your local government still needs to make?

Close to Home

Here is something you might like to do.

Check with your police department, fire department, or mayor's office. Ask if someone will visit your class. Have that person give you examples of local laws about any of the following things.

1. Keeping pets
2. Making noise
3. Hanging out
4. Making fires for outdoor cooking
5. Washing cars or watering lawns
6. Driving and parking cars and trucks
7. Cutting down trees
8. Clearing the streets by a certain time at night
9. Riding bicycles, motorcycles, and trail bikes
10. Getting rid of garbage

unit 17

Who Makes Local Laws?

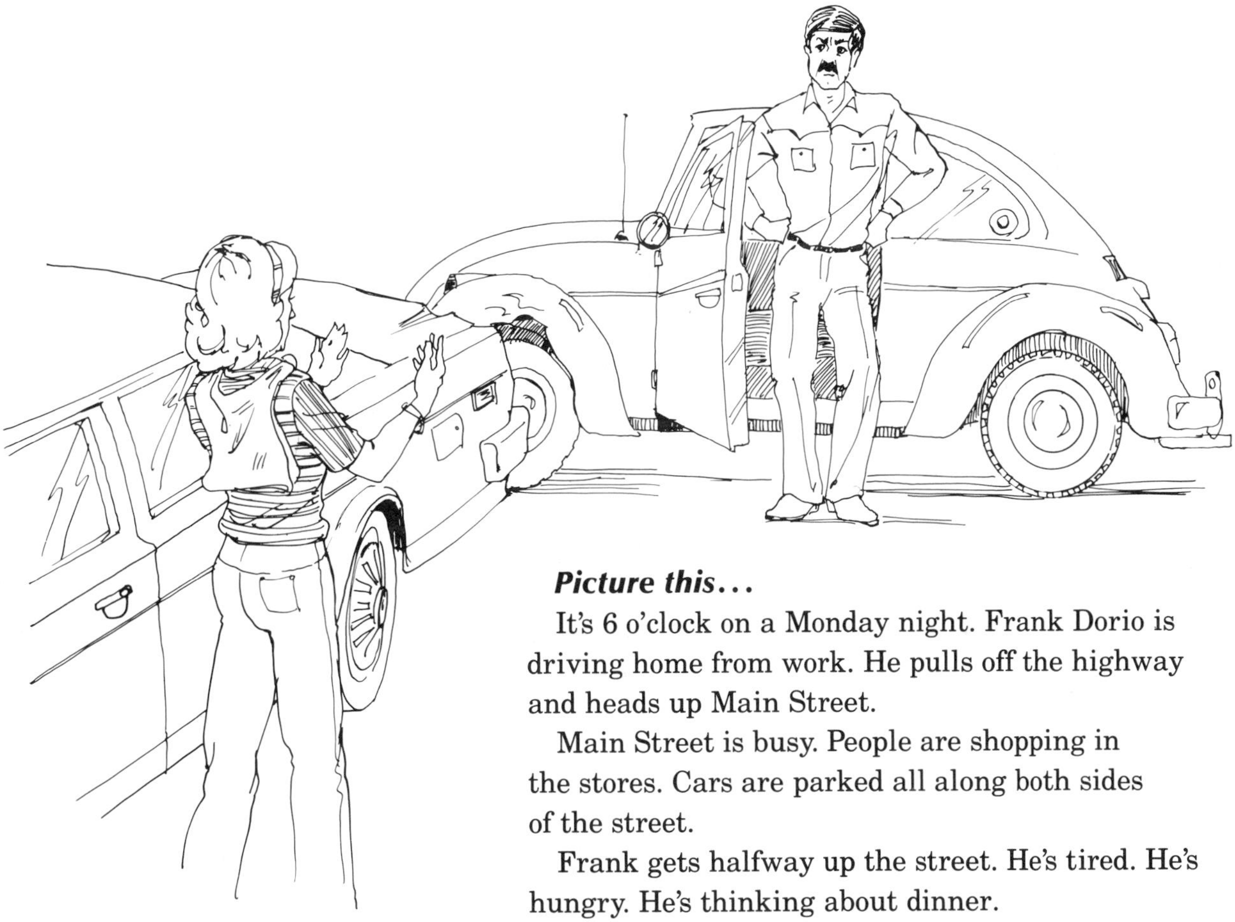

Picture this . . .

It's 6 o'clock on a Monday night. Frank Dorio is driving home from work. He pulls off the highway and heads up Main Street.

Main Street is busy. People are shopping in the stores. Cars are parked all along both sides of the street.

Frank gets halfway up the street. He's tired. He's hungry. He's thinking about dinner.

Suddenly a car backs out of a parking space and hits him. Frank feels the sudden jolt and hears the crunch of metal.

"Hey!" Frank shouts, stopping and getting out of his car. "What're you trying to do?"

"Sorry," the driver of the other car says. "I was in a hurry. I guess I didn't see you."

"A lot of good that does me!" Frank snaps. "Look what you did to my car!"

The Making of a Law

Accidents were happening every day on Main Street. Drivers were backing into the heavy flow of rush-hour traffic.

Many people in the city wanted a new parking law to solve the problem. The scenes that follow show how Frank and his neighbors got their **city council** to pass such a law. *Pass* means vote on and approve.

Scene 1: Decision to Act

NARRATOR: The time is 6:30 p.m. Frank Dorio has just come home. His wife, Anita, can see that he is angry.

ANITA: Something wrong, Frank?

FRANK: You bet there is! A busted headlight and a smashed fender!

ANITA: What happened?

FRANK: You know how the cars parked on Main Street are always backing into the traffic?

ANITA: Sure. They do it all the time.

FRANK: Well, some jerk backed out and hit me!

ANITA: That's the third time I've heard of that happening this week.

FRANK: I know. It happens every day.

ANITA: Then why don't you do something about it?

FRANK: Do something? Like what?

ANITA: Like get the city council to pass a law against parking on Main Street.

FRANK: How?

ANITA: Talk to some other people. There must be a lot of voters in this city who feel as you do.

FRANK: So what if there are?

ANITA: Well, if you all get together and go to the city council, maybe you can get a new law passed.

FRANK: Maybe you're right. I'll give it a try.

Scene 2: Neighborhood Meeting

NARRATOR: The scene is the Dorio kitchen, one week later. Some neighbors have come to talk with Frank and Anita about a new parking law. They and the Dorios are trying to decide what to do.

FRANK: OK. So we all agree on what the new law should be. Right?

GEORGE: Right. No parking on Main Street.

KAY: You really think we can get the city council to pass it?

GEORGE: Why not? We all want it, don't we? And we vote for the people on the council. So they have to do what we want.

KAY: No, they don't.

GEORGE: Why not?

KAY: Because there might be a lot of other people in the city who want to park on Main Street.

ANITA: Kay is right. Shoppers like to park there so that they can be close to the stores.

KAY: And the store owners will be against us. They want people to be able to park nearby so that more people will come to their stores.

FRANK: OK. So the shoppers and the store owners will be against us. But I still think there will be a lot of people on our side. People who drive on Main Street to get to and from work will agree with us.

KAY: I guess you're right. I know a lot of people are upset about the accidents.

GEORGE: And about how long it takes to drive down Main Street, even without accidents.

KAY: Right. So what's the next step?

FRANK: The next step is to talk over our ideas with the city council.

GEORGE: When?

FRANK: Tuesday night, when the council meets at city hall.

Scene 3: City Council Hearing

NARRATOR: The Dorios and their neighbors talked to the city council. They told the council about their idea for a new parking law. The council members said they would hold a hearing in two weeks to see how others felt about a new parking law. The hearing is about to begin.

MAYOR CRUZ: We're all here tonight to try to solve our traffic problem on Main Street. Will you begin, Mr. Dorio?

FRANK: Well, there's not much we can do about rush-hour traffic. But the cars parked in front of the stores cause most of the trouble.

COUNCILWOMAN STEIN: How is that, Mr. Dorio?

FRANK: First, parked cars take up too much space on the street. Without them, we could have another lane of traffic. Second, drivers back out into the heavy flow of traffic. That slows things up and causes accidents.

COUNCILMAN BROWN: So you want us to pass a law that would **ban** parking on Main Street?

FRANK: Yes. And so do a lot of other people.

STORE OWNER: Hey, wait a minute! That's not fair! What about the people who want to shop in the stores on Main Street?

SHOPPER: That's right! How about us?

FRANK: There's a city parking lot on River Street. You can park there.

SHOPPER: But that's two blocks away!

FRANK: It won't hurt you to walk two blocks.

SHOPPER: Maybe not. But why should we have to?

FRANK: Because the city has a problem, and we're trying to solve it.

MAYOR CRUZ: All right, folks. I think we've heard enough for now. The city council will think about what you have said. And next week we'll decide what to do.

Scene 4: The Vote

NARRATOR: The time is one week later. The city council is meeting again at city hall.

MAYOR CRUZ: We all know that something has to be done about the accidents on Main Street.

COUNCILWOMAN STEIN: Yes. And I agree that what Mr. Dorio said makes sense. But if we ban parking on Main Street, the shoppers and the store owners won't like it.

MAYOR CRUZ: So what are we going to do?

COUNCILMAN BROWN: I've got an idea.

MAYOR CRUZ: Let's hear it.

COUNCILMAN BROWN: The problem happens during **rush hours**. Right?

COUNCILWOMAN STEIN: Right.

COUNCILMAN BROWN: And rush hours are from 7 to 9 in the morning and 5 to 7 at night.

MAYOR CRUZ: OK. So what?

COUNCILMAN BROWN: So why don't we ban parking on Main Street during those hours *only*? That way we can solve the problem and still be fair to everyone.

MAYOR CRUZ: That makes sense.

COUNCILWOMAN STEIN: I agree.

MAYOR CRUZ: OK. It's time for a vote. Everyone in favor of banning parking on Main Street during rush hours raise your hand. (Everyone raises a hand.) Well, looks like Mr. Dorio will get his parking law.

Let's review the steps Frank and his neighbors took to get a new law passed.

1. They decided on what was needed.
2. They presented their idea to the city council.
3. The council held a hearing.
4. The council passed a new law that would solve the problem and still be fair to everyone.

Informed Citizen

Facts First

Choose the right word or words from the Word List to complete each sentence below.

Word List

city hall rush hours
parking hearing
city council

1. The Dorios and their neighbors wanted a new ______________ law.
2. They presented their idea to the ______________.
3. To make sure that everyone got a chance to tell his or her side, the council held a ______________.
4. The place where the council met is called ______________.
5. The council decided to pass a law that would ban parking only during the morning and evening ______________ .

Beyond the Facts

Here are some questions to think and talk about.

1. Suppose there were no local governments. Suppose all laws were made in state capitals or in the nation's capital. Would Frank have had an easier or a harder time getting a new parking law? Why?
2. Suppose you and your classmates, family, or friends wanted a new law to solve some local problem. How would you go about trying to get that law passed?
3. Why is it important that a town or city council hear from many people before it passes a new law?

Close to Home

Here are some things you might like to do.

1. Find out when and where your town or city council meets. Plan to attend a meeting. Later, invite a council member to visit your class. Have lots of questions ready to ask.
2. Make a scrapbook. Cut out newspaper stories about local laws and about the work of your town or city council. Paste them in your scrapbook. Talk about these stories with classmates, family, and friends.

unit 18

Who Runs Local Governments?

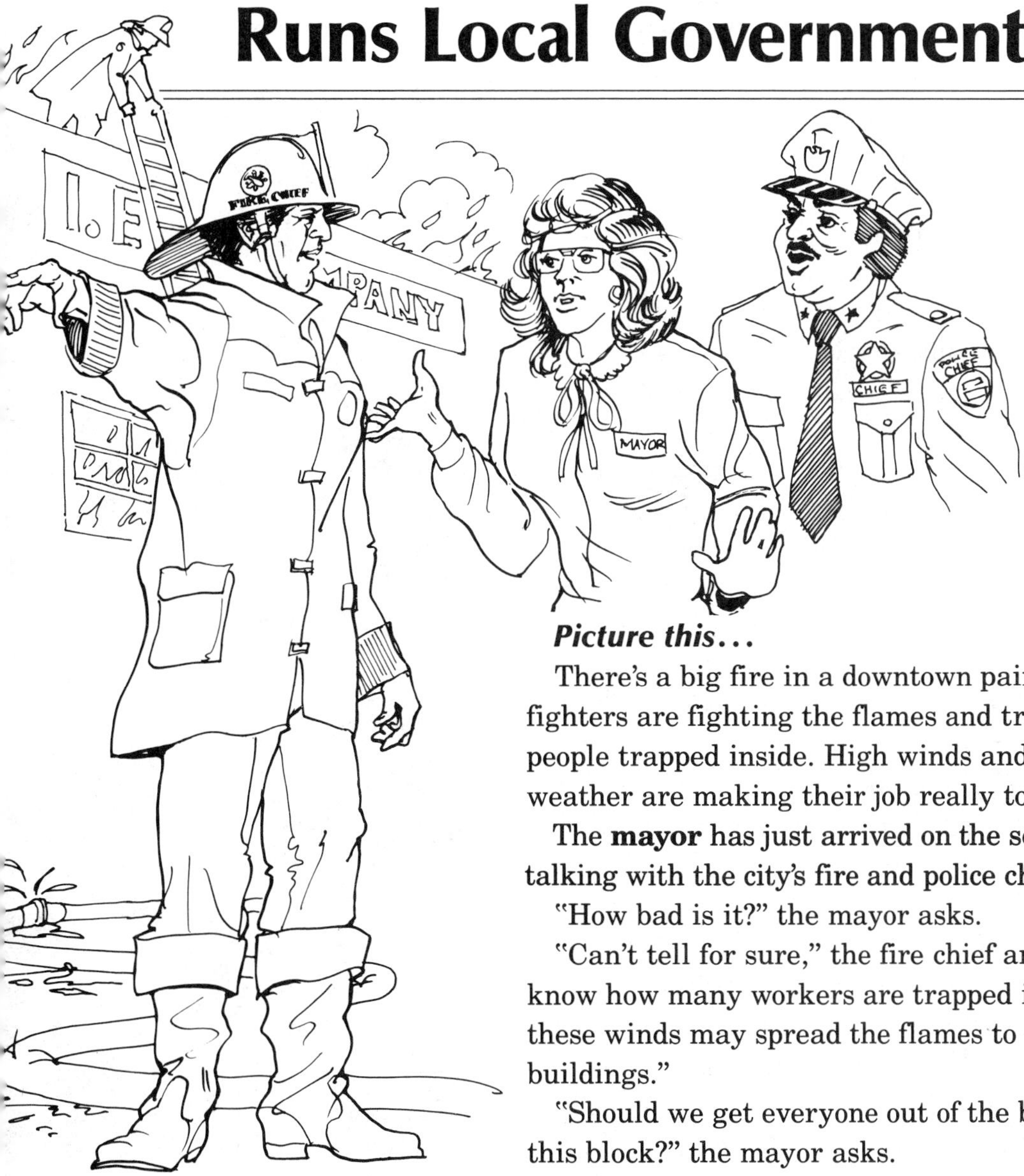

Picture this...

There's a big fire in a downtown paint factory. Fire fighters are fighting the flames and trying to rescue people trapped inside. High winds and freezing weather are making their job really tough.

The **mayor** has just arrived on the scene. She is talking with the city's fire and police chiefs.

"How bad is it?" the mayor asks.

"Can't tell for sure," the fire chief answers. "I don't know how many workers are trapped inside. And these winds may spread the flames to other buildings."

"Should we get everyone out of the buildings on this block?" the mayor asks.

"Yes, I think we'd better," answers the fire chief.

The mayor turns to the police chief. She says, "OK, chief, tell your officers to clear these buildings. I'll call for some buses to carry the people to a school. Meanwhile, get those trapped people out."

"Right!" say the chiefs at the same time.

Local Government Executives

In many towns and cities, a mayor heads the executive branch of government. But this is not true everywhere. Here are three ways local government may be run.

Mayor

In many large cities, a mayor is elected, or chosen, by the people. Sometimes the mayor has a lot of power. Such mayors are called "strong" mayors.

Strong mayors appoint people like the police chief and the fire chief. They help make the city's laws. And they see that the city laws are carried out and enforced.

One of the most important jobs the strong mayor has is to plan the city's budget. A budget is a plan for spending money. The mayor must also figure out where to get money to

- pay city workers;
- pave city streets and roads;
- get rid of garbage;
- run city buses and trains; and
- provide health care and low-cost housing for people with little or no income.

Mayors also take part in local events. A mayor may cut a ribbon at the opening of a new business. Or take part in a parade. Or make speeches at public meetings.

In some towns and cities, a mayor is not elected directly by the people. The people elect a council. Then the council chooses one of its members to serve as mayor.

The mayor then runs the meetings of the council and does the jobs we just talked about. But he or she has no more power than the other members of the council.

The mayor of San Francisco, Dianne Feinstein, rings the bell on a cable car. She is trying to raise money to help save the famous old cars.

The San Francisco Examiner

Mayor Feinstein visits a public place where vandals have done much damage. The mayor has to find ways to prevent and pay for such vandalism.

City Manager

Some city governments are run by a city manager instead of a mayor. City managers are hired by the city council to do many of the things a mayor might do.

The city manager acts as the city's chief executive. *Chief executive* means head of the executive branch. He or she may

- appoint, or name, department heads, such as the police and fire chiefs;
- see that city laws are carried out and enforced; and
- prepare the city's budget.

Commissioners

Some cities are run by a group of **commissioners**. The commissioners are elected by the voters of the city. Each commissioner is the head of a city department, such as the police department or the fire department. As such, he or she helps provide services and enforce the laws of the city.

The commissioners also meet as a group to help make the city's laws. In other words, they do the job that a town or city council would do.

County and District Executives

Counties and special districts, such as school districts, are run like towns and cities. Instead of a council, they have a board of supervisors or a board of education. *Board* means the same as *council*.

The board usually has five to seven members, elected by the people. The board members hire someone to run things from day to day. For example, a board of education hires a **superintendent** of schools. That person is then the boss of all the teachers and principals in the school district.

Local Departments

The work of local governments is done by different groups of people. These groups are called departments. Each department takes care of a different service. For example, the police department protects lives and property. The fire department puts out fires and helps save the lives of people in danger.

Here are some other departments that many local governments have.

Health

The health department employs doctors, nurses, and other health workers to run government hospitals and **clinics**. *Clinics* are places where people can get free or low-cost medical care.

Inspectors from the health department make sure that milk and water are safe to drink. They also inspect restaurants to see that they are clean and that the food is safe to eat.

Library

Most towns and cities have at least one public **library** where people can go to read and borrow books. Many libraries also have records, tapes, and films.

Public Works and Planning

The **public works** department builds and cares for streets and city buildings.

The **planning** department studies how to improve government services to different sections of counties, cities, and towns.

Courtesy Santa Clara County

A health inspector checks food at a restaurant. What do you suppose she looks for?

Recreation

Most towns and cities have a **recreation** department. This department builds and runs parks, pools, and trails for walking, hiking, jogging, biking, or horseback riding.

Some recreation departments also run community centers. People come to the centers to take classes, learn new crafts, and see shows.

Sanitation and Water

The **sanitation** department helps keep a town or city healthy and clean. The department's trucks pick up garbage. They sweep and wash streets. And they may remove snow from the streets in winter.

The water department supplies clean drinking water. It may also get rid of waste water.

Transportation

At one time, most local bus lines were privately owned. The same was true for other forms of local **transportation**, such as subway trains and ferries. Today, most public transportation lines are owned and run by local governments.

Welfare

Many people have little or no income. **Welfare** departments help these people meet their needs for food, clothing, shelter, and medical care.

Informed Citizen

Facts First

Match the words on the left with the person or group on the right that the words tell about.

1. Elected by the people to run city government
2. Hired by the city council to run city government
3. Heads a city department and helps make city laws

a. Commissioner
b. Mayor
c. City manager

4. Runs city hospitals
5. Gets rid of garbage
6. Runs buses, trains, and ferries

d. Transportation department
e. Health department
f. Sanitation department

Beyond the Facts

Here are some questions to think and talk about.

1. What are some local government services that you and your family use often?
2. What kind of executive does your town or city government have—a mayor, a manager, commissioners, or a combination?
3. More and more cities are being run by hired managers instead of elected mayors. Why might this be so?

Close to Home

Here is something you might like to do.

Find out what departments your local government has. You can do this by looking in the White Pages of your phone book.

Make a list of the departments that interest you. Call, write, or visit their main offices. Or invite someone from one or more departments to talk to your class.

unit 19

What Do Local Courts Do?

Picture this . . .

It's about 9 o'clock in the morning. Sam Jones is driving to work. He's late and in a hurry.

Sam turns off Park Street and zooms down 25th Avenue. A police officer stops Sam before he gets to the corner.

"OK," the police officer says. "Let's see your driver's license."

"What did I do?" Sam asks as he hands over his license.

"You were speeding," the officer replies.

"But I was only doing 35 miles an hour," Sam says.

"I know that," says the officer as he writes the ticket. "But this is a hospital zone. The speed limit here is 15 miles an hour."

"I'm sorry, officer," Sam says. "But I didn't see the road sign and I—"

"Don't tell me," the officer says, handing Sam the speeding ticket. "Tell it to the judge."

Traffic Court

Picture this...

It's Monday morning in traffic court. The court handles local traffic cases. The officer of the court calls the first case. "The state of California," he says, "**versus** Sam Jones." *Versus* means against.

Sam gets up and stands in front of the judge's bench.

"What is the **charge**?" the judge asks.

"Driving 35 miles an hour in a hospital zone," answers the officer.

"How do you **plead**?" the judge asks Sam. "Guilty, or not guilty?"

Sam knows he really doesn't have a good excuse. So he answers, "Guilty, Your Honor."

"Very well," says the judge. "You are fined $60."

Fair Trial

People who get traffic tickets are being accused of breaking a law. They have the right to a fair trial. They can get that trial in traffic court, but without a jury. The judge hears and decides each case alone.

Think back to when Sam got his speeding ticket. Suppose, at that time, he did not agree that he was going 35 miles per hour. Or suppose he really didn't know there was a hospital nearby. What if a truck had been blocking the traffic sign that said "Hospital Zone"?

Then Sam could have pleaded "not guilty" or "guilty with an explanation" when he was in court. The judge would have listened to Sam's explanation. If the judge believed Sam, she might have dismissed the case. Or she might have given Sam a lower fine.

Small Claims Court

Another court that handles local problems is small claims court. Here is the kind of case it might handle.

Case of the Broken TV

Rita Lopez is having a party. She's dancing with Pete Choy. Pete accidently bumps into Larry Miller. Larry gets upset and starts swinging.

Before anyone can stop him, Larry knocks over Rita's TV set. *Smash* goes the glass! The fight breaks up and so does the party.

During the next week, Rita has her TV set fixed. It costs her $150. She pays the money and keeps the bill.

Larry Won't Pay

Rita calls Larry and says he owes her $150.

"No way!" Larry says. "It was an accident."

"Accident or not," Rita answers, "you started the fight, and you knocked over the TV. I've got **witnesses** to prove it."

"I don't care what you have," Larry says. "I won't pay."

Larry hangs up.

Rita is angry. If you were Rita, what would you do?

Rita goes to small claims court and **files** a claim against Larry Miller. Small claims court handles disputes where the amount of money involved is usually under $1,500. The amount may be different in your state.

There is no jury in small claims court. A judge hears and decides each case alone.

Lopez versus Miller

Rita's case comes up in court. Several people who were at the party are there, including Larry Miller.

"The case of Lopez versus Miller," says the judge. "Are you ready to begin?"

Rita goes to the witness stand and swears to tell the truth. Then she tells what happened on the night of the party.

"Do you have any proof that what you're saying is true?" asks the judge.

"I do, Your Honor," Rita replies. "I have the bill from the repair shop. And I have witnesses."

"Let me see the bill, and let's hear from the witnesses," says the judge.

Each witness swears to tell the truth. And each witness tells the same story as Rita told: Larry started the fight and knocked over the TV set.

Larry's Turn

The next person on the witness stand is Larry Miller. Larry swears to tell the truth. Then the judge listens as Larry tells his side of the story. When Larry is done, the judge says, "You may step down, Mr. Miller."

The judge thinks for a minute. Then he says, "It is the decision of this court that you, Larry Miller, *did* start the fight and *did* knock over the TV set belonging to Rita Lopez. Therefore, the court orders you to pay the full cost of repairs."

Soon after, Rita gets a check from Larry for $150.

Other Local Courts

Traffic court and small claims court are part of your state court system. These courts are run by the state, but they handle local problems. Here are some other state courts that handle local problems.

Family Court

Most large cities have a special court that deals with family problems. This court is usually called family court.

Most of the cases this court handles involve **divorce** or **legal separation**. In such cases, the judge may decide how the family property should be divided. The judge may also decide which parent should take care of the children and how the children should be supported.

Juvenile Court

Juvenile court handles cases involving **minors** who are accused of breaking the law. In most states a minor is a person under 18 years old.

The purpose of this court is to help young lawbreakers become good citizens. Juvenile court judges have the power to send young lawbreakers to special schools or work camps instead of to prison.

Justices of the Peace

Some small towns have a **justice of the peace**. The justice of the peace is elected by the voters of the town. He or she does things a judge would do.

A justice of the peace handles cases that deal with traffic laws, disturbing the peace, local health laws, and other matters. He or she also has the power to perform wedding ceremonies.

Informed Citizen

Facts First

Choose the best word or words to complete each sentence below.

1. If you get a speeding ticket, you may have to go to
   a. small claims court.
   b. a probation officer.
   c. traffic court.
2. If someone owes you money and won't pay, you may be able to get help from
   a. family court.
   b. small claims court.
   c. a traffic officer.
3. Small claims courts don't have
   a. witnesses.
   b. judges.
   c. juries.
4. Cases of divorce or legal separation are usually handled by
   a. traffic court.
   b. family court.
   c. a justice of the peace.
5. Young people who are arrested usually go to
   a. family court.
   b. traffic court.
   c. juvenile court.
6. In many small towns, some court matters are handled by a
   a. probation officer.
   b. traffic officer.
   c. justice of the peace.

Beyond the Facts

Here are some questions to think and talk about.

1. Have you or has someone you know ever been to traffic, small claims, family, or juvenile court? If so, tell the class what it was like. (But do this only if you feel comfortable talking about it.)
2. Why do you think we have a special court for young people accused of breaking laws?
3. What do you think a person must be able to do in order to be a good and fair judge?

Close to Home

Here is something you might like to do.

Find out what courts—traffic, small claims, family, or juvenile—are nearby. Visit one or more of them. When you visit, watch and listen carefully to learn what goes on and who does what.

Back in class, make up a story or play about people in court. Write it by yourself, in a small group, or with the whole class. Draw pictures to add to the story or play. Or cut out pictures from magazines.

After you have written your story or play, act it out with other members of your group or class.

unit 20

What Are State Laws About?

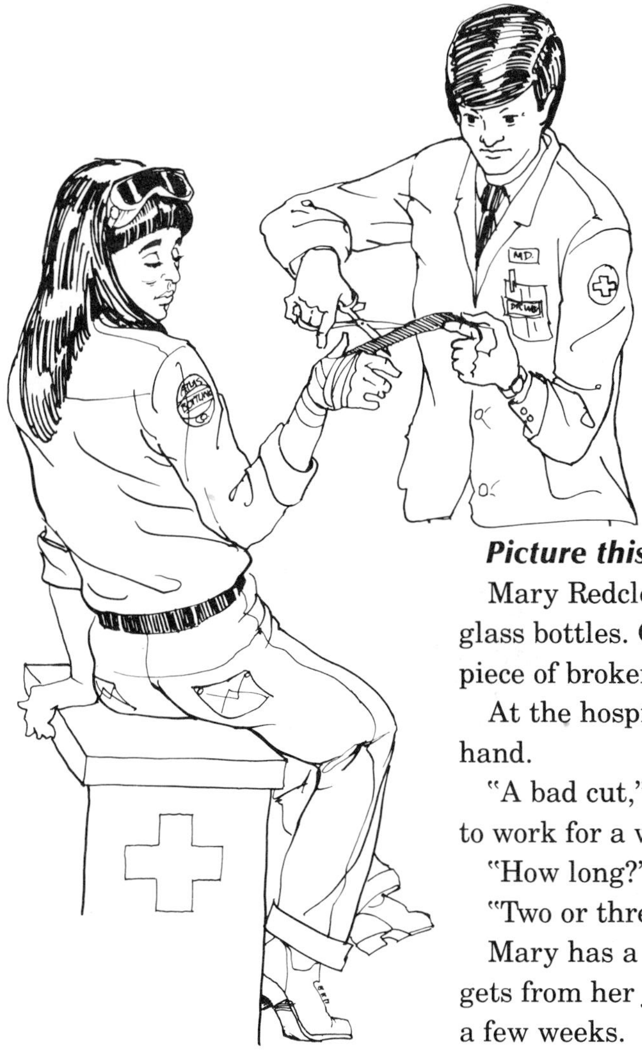

Picture this . . .

Mary Redcloud works in a factory that makes glass bottles. One day, Mary cuts her hand on a piece of broken glass.

At the hospital, the doctor stitches up Mary's hand.

"A bad cut," the doctor says. "You won't be able to work for a while."

"How long?" Mary asks.

"Two or three weeks," the doctor says.

Mary has a problem. She needs the money she gets from her job. But she won't be able to work for a few weeks.

Where can Mary get the money to live on while she is unable to work?

Mary can collect **workers' compensation**. Workers' compensation is money a worker gets if he or she gets hurt on the job and can't work for a while.

The San Jose Mercury News

Some jobs are more dangerous than others. But a worker can get hurt on almost any job.

Work Laws

All states have laws about work. Let's look at some of those laws.

Workers' Compensation

Some jobs are dangerous. A worker can get hurt. The worker may be hurt so badly that he or she can't work. That becomes a problem for both the worker and the employer.

Should the employer have to pay the worker while the worker isn't able to work? If not, what will the worker live on?

Workers' compensation helps solve the problem. State laws say that employers and workers must pay a certain amount of money into a workers' compensation **fund** every payday. Then, if a worker gets hurt on the job and cannot work for a while, he or she will be paid from this fund.

Unemployment Insurance

State laws also help people who lose their jobs. If these people can't find other jobs right away, they get checks from the government. The checks stop when the person finds a new job, or at the end of a certain number of weeks.

The money for these checks comes from an **unemployment** insurance fund. Both workers and employers pay money into that fund.

Other Work Laws

Your state has other laws about working. One of them tells how old you must be to have a full-time job. Another tells how old you must be to take a night job.

In your state, how old must you be to have a full-time job?

Picture this . . .

Jose is 21 years old and Kathy is 17. They've been going steady for over a year now. And they want to get married. But Kathy's mother is against it.

"Kathy's too young," her mother says. "She's only 17."

"But we love each other," Jose says. "And you can't stop us."

Do you think Kathy's mother can stop them from getting married?

If you said yes, you'd probably be right. Why? Because the law in most states says that Kathy's too young to get married without her parents' **consent**. *Consent* means OK.

Marriage Laws

Every state has laws about marriage. These laws set the age at which a person can get married. In most states you have to be at least 18—unless you have the consent of your parents.

States also have laws about caring for children and about ending a marriage by divorce or separation.

Other State Laws

States have many other kinds of laws. There are laws about health, business, drinking, gambling, and many other things. Two groups of laws that may interest you are those dealing with autos and school.

Auto Laws

Most states have a law about how old a person has to be before he or she can get a driver's license. And to get that license, a person has to pass a test. The test shows if a person knows the state's traffic laws.

State governments also set speed limits on state highways. They set limits on how big and how heavy a truck can be to travel on certain highways.

Other state auto laws are about safety and pollution control. And some states have laws about car insurance.

School Laws

Every state has laws about who has to go to school. In most states, you have to be at least 16 years old before you can leave school. And in some states, if you leave school at 16, you still have to finish high school by taking special classes.

Peterbilt Motors Company

If you owned and drove this truck, what state laws do you think would affect you?

Informed Citizen

Facts First

Choose the right word from the Word List to complete each sentence below.

Word List

insurance	compensation
full-time	traffic
consent	school

1. Money paid to a worker who has been hurt on the job is called workers' __________________ .
2. Money paid to a worker who has lost his or her job is called unemployment __________________ .
3. States also have laws about how old you must be before you can have a __________________ job.
4. In most states, a person under 18 needs the __________________ of his or her parents in order to get married.
5. Before people can get a driver's license, they have to show that they know most of the state's __________________ laws.
6. In most states, you must be at least 16 before you can leave __________________ .

Beyond the Facts

Here are some questions to think and talk about.

1. What age do you have to be in your state to
   a. work full-time?
   b. leave school?
   c. get a driver's license?
   d. buy beer, wine, or liquor?
   e. get married without parents' consent?
2. Why do you think states have laws about how old people must be to do each of those things?
3. Do you think such laws are fair? Why or why not?

Close to Home

Here are some things you might like to do.

1. If you don't know the answer to any part of question 1 in **Beyond the Facts**, find out what the answer is. Ask at your local police department or sheriff's office.
2. Find out about any of the following things that interest you:
   a. How do you get a driver's license?
   b. How do you get a marriage license?
   c. How do you get a work permit?

   Ask your teacher, counselor, or librarian to tell you where you can find this information.

unit 21

Who Makes State Laws?

Picture this...

It's a Saturday afternoon. Greg Lee is riding down Elm Street on his motorcycle. Clear sky. Warm sun. He can't wait to reach the open highway.

Suddenly a dog runs into the street in front of the motorcycle. Greg twists the front wheel and squeezes the brakes. The motorcycle bucks. Greg flies off.

A man and a woman run out from their yard. They see that Greg's head is bleeding.

"Call an ambulance!" the man shouts to his wife.

Soon an ambulance comes and takes Greg to a hospital.

"That guy is lucky he's alive," the woman says. "He should have been wearing a helmet."

"You said it!" the man replies. "In fact, there ought to be a law to make motorcycle riders wear helmets."

Who do you think would make such a law?

State Lawmakers

Accidents like the one you read about on page 134 happen every day. So some state **legislatures** have passed helmet laws. Let's see how legislatures work.

Two Houses

In 49 of the states, the legislature is divided into two houses, or groups. One house is called the senate. The other house is usually called the house of representatives.

The only state that does not have two houses is Nebraska. Nebraska's lawmakers meet in a single group.

Committees

State legislatures deal with hundreds of bills every year. A bill is an idea for a law, written in a special way.

Bills cover so many different subjects that no lawmaker has enough time to learn everything about all of them. So what do you think the lawmakers do?

The lawmakers work in small groups called committees. Each committee handles only a certain kind of bill. One committee might handle bills about driving. Another might handle bills about education, business, or health.

Each committee decides which of its bills are the most important. Then the committee members study each of those bills. They hold hearings where they listen to the opinions of experts and other concerned citizens.

Finally, the members of the committee vote on each bill. If the committee passes the bill, it sends that bill to all the other members of the legislature for a vote.

From Bill to Law

Every new law begins as a bill. Most bills are **introduced**, or started, by members of the legislature.

A bill can be introduced in either house of the legislature. But to become a law, a bill must be passed by both houses (except in Nebraska).

In a state's house of representatives, a lawmaker usually introduces a bill by dropping it into a box on the desk of the house clerk. The bill then goes to the speaker of the house, who assigns it to the right committee. Senate bills are introduced in a similar way.

Committee Hearing

As you read on page 135, the committee studies the bill, holds hearings, and then votes. If the committee passes the bill, it sends the bill to the house (or the senate) for a vote.

Vote

The house of representatives (or the senate) discusses the bill and then votes on it. If more than half the lawmakers pass the bill, it goes to the other house for a vote. When the bill has been passed by both houses, it is sent to the **governor**.

Role of the Governor

If the governor signs the bill, it becomes a law. But the governor may not like the bill. In such cases, the governor may veto it. That means he or she may refuse to sign the bill.

When that happens, the bill goes back to the legislature and must be voted on again. This time, if at least two-thirds of the members vote for the bill, it becomes a law.

Motorcycle Safety Law

The four scenes that follow show how a bill about safety helmets becomes a law.

Scene 1: Introducing the Bill

NARRATOR: The scene is the state house of representatives. Representative Jones drops a bill into a box on the house clerk's desk.

CLERK: What's this one about, Mr. Jones?

REPRESENTATIVE JONES: Motorcycle safety.

CLERK: Is this the one that will make motorcycle riders wear safety helmets?

REPRESENTATIVE JONES: That's right.

CLERK: It's about time we had a bill like that.

REPRESENTATIVE JONES: Well, let's hope we can get it passed.

Scene 2: The Committee Hearing

NARRATOR: The scene is a committee room in the state house of representatives. A safety expert is speaking for the new safety bill. The committee members are asking her questions.

REPRESENTATIVE ADAMS: What good will this new law do?

SAFETY EXPERT: It will cut down the number of deaths and bad injuries from motorcycle accidents.

REPRESENTATIVE ADAMS: How?

SAFETY EXPERT: Most deaths in motorcycle accidents are caused by head injuries. This helmet law would help protect motorcycle riders from head injuries in accidents.

REPRESENTATIVE POLASKI: That makes sense.

REPRESENTATIVE HO: I agree. The main thing is to save lives.

Scene 3: The House Vote

NARRATOR: The scene is a big room in the house of representatives. The committee has finished studying the bill. Now all the people in the state house of representatives are waiting to vote on it.

SPEAKER: The house will now come to order. It is time for debate on house bill 5421 about motorcycle safety helmets.

NARRATOR: Members speak for and against the bill. Then the speaker of the house calls for a vote.

SPEAKER: All those in favor of the bill please raise your hand.

CLERK: *(counting)* 85 votes for the bill.

SPEAKER: All those against the bill please raise your hand.

CLERK: *(counting)* 15 votes against the bill. The bill passes by a vote of 85 to 15!

Scene 4: The Governor Decides

NARRATOR: The scene is the governor's office. The governor is with his secretary. He has just read the motorcycle safety bill. The bill has passed in both houses of the state legislature. But before it can become a law, the governor must sign it.

SECRETARY: Do you think this bill really will help save lives?

GOVERNOR: That's what the experts say.

SECRETARY: I know. But a lot of motorcycle owners won't like it.

GOVERNOR: That's true. But it will help protect them.

SECRETARY: So you're going to sign it?

GOVERNOR: Yes. I think, with more and more people riding motorcycles, we need this law.

Four Steps

The motorcycle safety bill became a law by going through these four steps:

1. The bill was introduced in the house of representatives.
2. The bill went to a committee that held hearings and voted on it.
3. The bill was passed by the house of representatives and then by the senate.
4. The bill was signed by the governor.

Informed Citizen

Facts First

Decide if each statement below is true or false. If you think it is false, be ready to tell why you think so.

True or False?

1. All states except Nebraska have two houses, or groups, of state lawmakers.
2. An idea for a law is called a veto.
3. Bills are usually studied by committees before they are voted on by the house or the senate.
4. If a committee votes against a bill, the bill is not sent to the house or the senate for a vote.
5. In those states that have two groups of lawmakers, a bill must be passed by both groups before it is sent to the governor.
6. If the governor doesn't like a bill, he or she has to sign it anyway.
7. If the governor doesn't like a bill, it cannot become a law.

Beyond the Facts

Here are some questions to think and talk about.

1. Why might some people be against a motorcycle helmet safety law?
2. How does the making of a state law differ from the making of a town or city law?
3. It is not easy to get a bill passed into law on the state level of government. Do you think this is good or bad? Why?

Close to Home

Here are some things you might like to do.

1. Check local newspapers and news shows for stories about the work of your state legislature or assembly. Cut out the newspaper stories to add to your scrapbook. Talk about the news stories with classmates, family, and friends.
2. Find out who your state representatives and senators are. The library can help you get this information. Decide on some things that you would like to tell or ask these people. Form a few committees. Have each committee write a letter to a different state representative or senator.

unit 22

Who Runs State Governments?

Picture this...

The place is a state prison. The man behind bars has been in prison for ten years. He has another ten years to go.

The prisoner has become a better person. He is willing and able to obey the law and help others. The prisoner's lawyer has asked the governor to free him now.

The governor's answer will come today. The prisoner walks up and down his cell. He's waiting for the answer. Suddenly he hears the sound of footsteps in the hall. A guard is coming. Behind him is the lawyer. The prisoner holds his breath and waits.

The guard and the lawyer reach the prisoner's cell.

"What did the governor say?" the prisoner asks.

"You're in luck," the lawyer answers. "The governor is going to set you free!"

The Governor Is in Charge

The governor's main job is to see that the laws of the state are carried out and enforced. But he or she has the power to **pardon**, or forgive, people who break the law. Or the governor can shorten the time they must spend in prison.

Other Powers of the Governor

Here are some other powers the governor has. The governor can

- appoint the heads of state departments;
- **propose**, or suggest, bills for the legislature to consider;
- veto bills he or she does not approve of; and
- call out the National Guard to stop **riots** or help people during floods, fires, or other **disasters**.

Term of Office

The governor of the state is elected by the voters of the state. In a few states the governor serves for a **term** of two years. In most states the governor serves for a term of four years.

Members of the Indiana National Guard help clean up fallen logs after a tornado. Who do you think ordered them into action?

U.S. Army Photograph

Other State Executives

The governor has many people who help him or her run the state government. In most states these people are elected by the voters of the state. Each of these people has a special job to do.

Lieutenant Governor

Many states have a **lieutenant** governor. He or she acts for the governor if the governor is away.

The lieutenant governor takes the governor's place if the governor dies, resigns, or is removed from office. In many states, the lieutenant governor is also the head of the state senate and can vote on a bill in case of a **tie vote**. A tie vote is when there are as many lawmakers for a bill as there are against it.

Secretary of State

The secretary of state keeps the state's records. He or she also **issues**, or gives, licenses to businesses, doctors, lawyers, and others.

Attorney General

The **attorney general** is the chief lawyer for the state. He or she is in charge of all the lawyers who represent the state in court. And he or she is the state's chief **legal advisor**. That is, the attorney general helps state officials understand and use laws and courts.

Treasurer

The state **treasurer** collects taxes and handles all the money coming into and going out of the state treasury.

Departments

The work that a state government does is divided among different departments. Here are some of the departments found in most states. These departments may have different names in your state.

Department	What the Department Does
Business and Labor	○ Makes rules about doing business ○ Helps workers
Conservation	○ Protects the state's water supply, forests, and wildlife
Education	○ Sets up state **colleges** and **universities** ○ Helps local governments run public schools
Employment	○ Helps people find jobs ○ Runs an unemployment insurance program
Health	○ Runs state hospitals and does medical **research**
Motor Vehicles	○ Issues driver's licenses and license plates
Public Utilities Commission	○ Sees that the rates charged by electric, gas, and telephone companies are fair
Public Works	○ Builds and takes care of state highways, bridges, and tunnels
State Police	○ Enforces state laws and helps local law enforcers
Welfare	○ Runs programs to help people with little or no income

State Budget

One of the main jobs of the governor is to make up a state budget. To do this, he or she has to meet with the heads of different departments. The scene that follows shows what a state budget meeting is like.

Budget Meeting

NARRATOR: The scene is the governor's office in the state capital. The governor is meeting with the heads of the employment, welfare, and public works departments. They are talking about next year's budget.

GOVERNOR: One of our biggest problems right now is unemployment. A lot of people are out of work in this state.

HEAD OF EMPLOYMENT DEPARTMENT: Yes. And that means we'll be paying out a lot of money in unemployment **benefits**.

HEAD OF WELFARE DEPARTMENT: That's right. And it also means more welfare checks than usual.

GOVERNOR: I know. But what about jobs? What can we do about finding jobs for some of these people?

HEAD OF PUBLIC WORKS DEPARTMENT: Well, the new state highway will help. We'll need workers to build it.

GOVERNOR: That's true. But what about our cities? I've gotten letters and phone calls from the mayors of a dozen cities. They all need more money.

HEAD OF EMPLOYMENT DEPARTMENT: That means we'll have to raise state taxes again.

GOVERNOR: I know. But the voters won't like it. So I'm not sure the state legislature will go along with it.

NARRATOR: After a number of meetings, the governor finally decides what needs to be done and how. Then he prepares the budget. The budget is sent to the state legislature for approval.

Which department builds highways, bridges, and tunnels?

Informed Citizen

Facts First

Match each job on the left with the person or department on the right that does that job.

1. Sees that state laws are carried out and enforced
2. Takes the governor's place when necessary
3. Collects taxes and pays out money
4. Keeps state records and issues licenses
5. Gives legal advice and is in charge of the state government's lawyers

a. Treasurer
b. Governor
c. Lieutenant governor
d. Attorney general
e. Secretary of state

6. Helps run schools and sets up state colleges
7. Helps people with little or no income
8. Builds and takes care of state highways

f. Public works department
g. Welfare department
h. Education department

Beyond the Facts

Here are some questions to think and talk about.

1. Why might a governor pardon a person who breaks the law?
2. In what ways is the job of a governor similar to the job of the President of the United States? In what ways is it different?
3. What is the name of your governor? What do you know about him or her?

Close to Home

Here is something you might like to do.

Watch local newspapers and news shows for stories about your governor, about other elected state officials, and about your state's departments. Cut out the newspaper stories and paste them in your scrapbook. Discuss the news stories with your classmates, family, and friends.

unit 23

What Do State Courts Do?

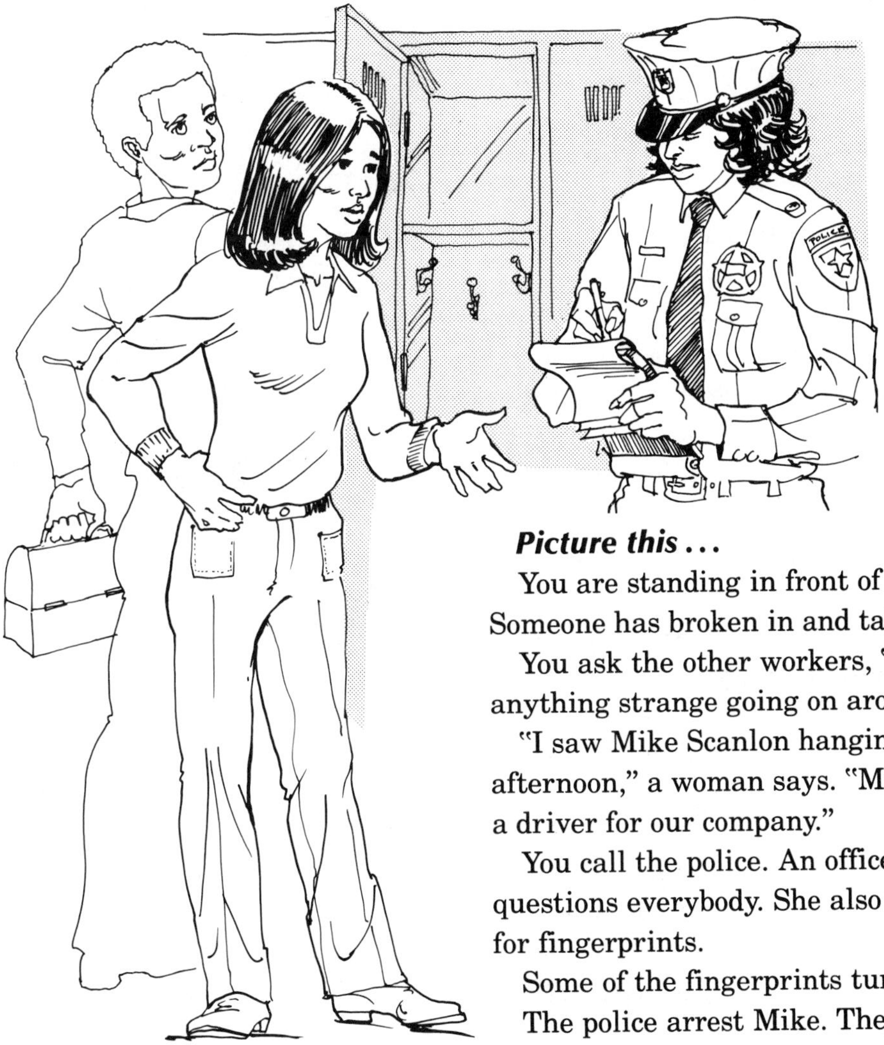

Picture this . . .

You are standing in front of your locker at work. Someone has broken in and taken your new watch.

You ask the other workers, "Did anyone see anything strange going on around the lockers?"

"I saw Mike Scanlon hanging around this afternoon," a woman says. "Mike used to be a driver for our company."

You call the police. An officer comes and questions everybody. She also checks your locker for fingerprints.

Some of the fingerprints turn out to be Mike's.

The police arrest Mike. They ask him where he put the watch.

"I didn't steal it," Mike answers.

"Then why were you hanging around the lockers?" an officer asks.

"To meet a friend," Mike answers. "That's all."

Do you think Mike is guilty, or not guilty?

Mike Goes to Criminal Court

It's really hard to tell if Mike is guilty or not, isn't it? And that's why we have courts. They are the fairest way to decide if someone is guilty or not.

Because Mike is charged with committing a crime, he'll go to a criminal court for trial. There, a jury of 12 people will decide if he is guilty or not guilty. You, of course, will be there too.

The Trial Begins

The judge enters the courtroom. His main job will be to make sure that Mike gets a fair trial.

To start, the lawyer for the **prosecution** presents her side of the case. She has to prove that Mike stole your watch. She calls witnesses to the stand—the police, people from your company, and you.

Then Mike's lawyer, the lawyer for the **defense**, has a turn. He tries to show that no one can tell for sure that Mike is guilty. The defense lawyer also calls witnesses—Mike's friend at the company, other workers who saw Mike, and Mike himself.

Both lawyers get time to **cross-examine**, or question, each other's witnesses. And the lawyers each have a turn at the end to review their side of the case.

The lawyer for the defense questions a witness.

The Jury Decides

Finally it's time for the members of the jury to decide if Mike is guilty or not guilty. The judge tells them to think carefully about all they have seen and heard before making their decision.

An officer takes the jury to another room and locks them in. There they stay and talk until they reach a decision called a verdict. Based on that verdict, Mike may go to prison or go free.

The jury decides Mike is guilty.

Picture this...

You are shopping in a supermarket. You are standing near the bread, trying to decide which kind to buy. A worker with a hand truck comes rushing towards you. The hand truck is loaded with heavy boxes.

The worker doesn't see you. He runs into you and knocks you down. You feel a sharp pain in your ankle.

It turns out that your ankle is broken and you cannot go to work for several weeks. You not only have doctor bills, but you lose some pay as well.

You ask the owner of the supermarket to pay your doctor bills and to make up for your lost pay. The owner refuses. What can you do?

You can **sue**!

Civil Courts

Sue means take someone to court to settle differences. The person who has a **complaint** is called the **plaintiff**. The one who is being sued is called the defendant.

In the case above, who do you think would be the plaintiff? Who would be the defendant?

Right. You would be the plaintiff. The store owner would be the defendant.

What happened was an accident, not a crime. Because there has been no crime, your **lawsuit** would be heard in a civil court rather than in a criminal court.

People take each other to court for all kinds of reasons. But most civil lawsuits involve accidents, poor service, property damage, or failure to pay bills.

For example, suppose one of the following things were to happen to you.

- You trip on a broken step in a neighbor's house and have to get medical care. Your neighbor refuses to pay the doctor bills. You might sue your neighbor.
- A delivery van backs into your car. The owner refuses to pay for repairs. You might sue the owner.
- You buy a tape recorder. It doesn't work right. The store owner refuses to fix it, give you a different one, or give your money back. You might sue the store owner.
- You own a business. One of your customers refuses to pay her bills. You might sue your customer.

Similar to Criminal Courts

Trials in a civil court are similar to ones in a criminal court. Usually, the defendant has the right to a trial by jury. Or the defendant may ask that a judge decide the case without a jury.

The defendant and the plaintiff each have a lawyer. The lawyers call witnesses, cross-examine each other's witnesses, and review their sides of the case. Finally, the judge or the jury decides on a verdict.

But in a civil court, the verdict will not be "guilty" or "not guilty." Instead, the case is decided either "in favor of the plaintiff" or "in favor of the defendant."

If the plaintiff wins, the defendant will have to pay the plaintiff in some way. The court decides what the payment should be.

If the plaintiff loses, he or she may have to pay the defendant's costs and the lawyer's fees. So plaintiffs should be sure they have a good chance of winning before they take anyone to court.

A jury is a group of people chosen from the community. The judge explains what they must do.

Picture this...

The jury in Mike Scanlon's trial finds Mike guilty. But Mike still says he is not guilty. And his lawyer believes him.

What can Mike and his lawyer do?

Mike, with the help of his lawyer, can appeal the jury's verdict. That is, Mike can ask the judges of a higher court, a court of appeals, to decide if the jury's verdict is fair.

Courts of Appeals

Courts in the United States are arranged in a system of low, middle, and high courts. Traffic courts are on the low end. Trial courts, like the one where Mike's case was heard, are in the middle. And courts of appeals are on the high end.

Decisions made in a trial court are not always final. If a higher court disagrees with a decision, it can reverse, or change, the verdict.

Here's how a court of appeals works.

The judges of the court of appeals decide whether or not there is a good reason for appeal. If there is, one or more judges from the court of appeals read a report of the trial. They may also listen to the lawyers from both sides of the case.

Finally, the judges make a decision. They may decide to agree with the verdict of the trial court. Or they may reverse the decision of the trial court.

In Mike's case, reversing the trial court's decision would mean saying that Mike was *not guilty* instead of *guilty*. In that case, Mike would go free.

But the appeals court might decide that a mistake was made in the trial court. Then there would be another trial.

Decisions made in civil cases may also be appealed.

Informed Citizen

Facts First

Choose the right word from the Word List to complete each sentence below.

Word List

plaintiff	defendant
verdict	criminal
appeal	reverse
civil	

1. The trials of people accused of crimes take place in ________________ courts.
2. The trials in which one person complains about another person take place in ________________ courts.
3. The person who has a complaint is called the ________________ .
4. The person who is being sued is called the ________________ .
5. The jury's decision at the end of a trial is called the ________________ .
6. If a defendant feels that he or she did not get a fair trial, the defendant may ask his or her lawyer to ________________ to a higher court.
7. The judges in a court of appeals have the power to ________________ the decision of a lower court.

Beyond the Facts

Here are some questions to think and talk about.

1. What are the differences between civil courts and criminal courts? Between trial courts and appeals courts?
2. Defendants in both civil and criminal trials have a choice. They may have a jury decide the case. Or they may have the judge decide. Most defendants choose to have a jury decide. Why do you think they do that?
3. What are some other ways that people might settle their differences besides going to civil courts?

Close to Home

Here are some things you might like to do.

1. Check your local newspaper for stories about trials. Cut them out for your scrapbook and paste them under the headings *Civil Cases* and *Criminal Cases*.
2. Visit a court while a trial is going on. Watch carefully to see what each person does at the trial.

   Later, hold a mock trial in class. Choose people to play all the parts.

unit 24

Who Pays the Bills?

Picture this . . .

Doris Fong works as a salesperson. She owns a six-room house on Maple Street. And she just got a letter from her local government.

"What is it?" her son asks.

"Taxes," Doris groans. "The taxes on the house are going up again."

"It's not fair," her son says. "Property taxes are already too high."

"I know," Doris says. "But what can we do? Somebody has to pay to keep the town running."

Local Revenues

It takes a lot of revenue to run your local government. Revenue is money that a government collects to pay its expenses. Schools, roads, fire trucks, and many other things have to be paid for. And all the people who work for your local government have to be paid.

Where do you think your local government gets the revenue to pay for all these things?

You usually have to get a permit from your local government before you can build a house. Once it's built, you have to pay a property tax on it every year.

Property Taxes

Most local revenue comes from property taxes. Property taxes are paid by people who own land, a house, or a place of business. This money is collected each year by your local government. And the money is used to pay for the services your local government provides.

Sales Taxes

Many local governments have a sales tax. This is a tax on goods and services.

Stores and other businesses may include the sales taxes in the prices marked on things they sell. Or they may add the taxes to the prices later—when you pay for the things you buy.

The stores and businesses turn over the money they collect for local sales taxes to their local governments.

Licenses and Permits

Another kind of revenue your local government collects is from people who want to start businesses. In most cities you have to get a license to start a business. You pay a certain amount of money to the city for the license. The license gives you the right to carry on your business.

The Daily Review

The San Francisco Examiner/John Storey

Money collected from parking meters helps pay the bills of local government.

If you want to build a factory, you have to get a building permit from the city. The permit gives you the right to put up the building.

You usually need a permit to build any kind of building, including a house. You may also need a permit if you want to add rooms on to a house.

Fines and Meters

A local government also collects money from people who break traffic and parking laws. People pay fines for things like speeding or driving through a red light. People are fined for parking in a "no parking" **zone**.

A city may also collect money from parking **meters**. All day long people park and put money in the meters. This can add up to a lot of money in a year's time.

State and Federal Aid

Local governments get extra money from the state each year. They also get some money from the federal government.

The money that a town or a city collects from all these things is used to pay its bills.

State Revenues

Your state government also needs a lot of money to keep it running. State highways, hospitals, parks, and many more things have to be paid for. And all the people who work for your state government have to be paid. Here are some of the ways that states get the revenue they need.

Picture this...

Joe Gorman got a job in an aircraft factory. The job pays $300 a week.

But Joe just got his first paycheck. And the amount on the check is only $250.

"Hey!" Joe says to a friend. "What happened to the rest of my money?"

Where do you think the rest of Joe's money went?

Part of it went to pay his federal taxes. That money goes to the federal, or national, government. Another part of Joe's pay went to pay for unemployment insurance. And a third part of Joe's pay went to pay his state income tax.

Income Taxes

Most states have an income tax. An income tax is a tax on the money you earn.

How much tax do you pay on your income? That depends on how much money you earn. The more money you earn, the more income tax you pay.

People who own businesses also pay income taxes. The amount of tax a business owner pays depends on how much money the business earns.

Does your state have an income tax?

Sales Taxes

Many states have a sales tax. As you read on page 154, this is a tax on goods and services.

Stores and other businesses may include the sales taxes in the prices marked on things they sell. Or they may add the taxes to the prices later—when you pay for the things you buy. The stores and businesses send the money they collect for state sales taxes to their state governments.

Courtesy California Department of Transportation

Drivers often have to pay tolls to use bridges, tunnels, and highways.

Fees and Tolls

State governments make car owners register their cars and get license plates. They charge a fee for that. A fee is a charge for some service.

States also collect money from drivers for using certain state highways and bridges. This money is called a **toll**.

What do you think the money from these fees and tolls is usually used for?

That's right. It's used to build and take care of state highways and bridges.

Federal Aid

Your state government gets extra money from the federal government each year. The state government uses some of this money to help pay its bills. And it passes some of the money on to local governments.

Informed Citizen

Facts First

Choose the best word or words to complete each sentence below.

1. Local governments get most of the revenue they need from
   a. income taxes.
   b. tolls.
   c. property taxes.
2. In most towns and cities, before you can build a new building, you must get a
   a. permit.
   b. meter.
   c. fine.
3. Towns and cities get some revenue from traffic fines and parking
   a. taxes.
   b. laws.
   c. meters.
4. Many state governments get revenue from
   a. income taxes.
   b. property taxes.
   c. parking fines.
5. Many state governments also have
   a. federal taxes.
   b. sales taxes.
   c. meter taxes.
6. State governments get some of their revenue from
   a. parking meters.
   b. license-plate fees and bridge tolls.
   c. building permits.

Beyond the Facts

Here are some questions to think and talk about.

1. What different kinds of local and state taxes do you and your family now pay?
2. What kinds of government services do you get in return for the taxes you pay?
3. How do you feel about having to pay taxes?

Close to Home

Here is something you might like to do.

With the help of your teacher, find answers to the questions below.

1. If your state has a sales tax, how much is it? Is there a local sales tax? If so, how much is it? What are some things this tax money pays for?
2. How much are the fees for a driver's license and license plates in your state? What is this money used for?
3. How much are the usual fines for speeding and illegal parking in your town or city? What is this money used for?

unit 25

How Do You Become a Voter?

Picture this...

There's a big election coming up. Governor Burns is running for a second term as governor. A woman named Nancy Morino is running against him. People all over the state are talking about the election.

"I think Burns is a good governor," one person says. "He built a new state highway, didn't he?"

"Sure," a second person says. "But he raised our gasoline tax and bridge tolls to do it! And what's he done about jobs? There are more people out of work now than when he became governor. I say it's time for a change."

These people have strong feelings about who should be governor. What can they do to help elect the person they want?

Right. They can vote in the upcoming election.

Who Can Vote?

Voting is one of the most important things an American citizen can do. Why? Because each person who votes helps to decide who will make our laws and who will run our government.

Voting Laws

To vote in the United States, you must

- be at least 18 years old;
- be a citizen of the United States; and
- live in the town or city where you want to vote.

In addition, you must not have a criminal record. A person who has been **convicted** of a serious crime loses his or her right to vote. *Convicted* means found guilty.

AP/Wide World Photos

A new voter registers to vote. How old do you have to be to vote in the United States?

Signing Up to Vote

New voters must register, or sign up, before they can vote.

When you want to register to vote, you go to the **registrar** of voters at your town hall or city hall. You ask for a voter **registration** form. On the form, you write your full name, your address, and your date of birth.

You may be asked to show proof of your age. What do you think you can use to prove your age?

Did you think of a **birth certificate**? A birth certificate is a form that tells where and when a person was born.

Do you or your parents have a copy of your birth certificate? If not, you can get one by visiting or writing the office of the town or city clerk in the place where you were born.

UPI/Bettmann Newsphotos

A group of new citizens are being sworn in. They are promising to be good citizens of the United States.

Citizenship

The law says that in order to vote you must be a citizen of the United States. What is a citizen and how do you become one?

Anyone born in the United States is a citizen. And a person born outside the United States is a citizen if at least one of his or her parents is a citizen.

Other people can become citizens of the United States. They must be at least 18 years old. They must have lived in the United States for at least five years. And they must

- read, write, and speak English;
- know about American history and government;
- find two United States citizens who will say good things about them; and
- promise to be good citizens.

Once a person meets all these conditions, he or she can get a set of citizenship papers. When registering to vote, the person can use these papers to prove that he or she is a citizen.

How about you? Are you a citizen of the United States? If not, you might want to ask your teacher to help you become one.

Going to the Polls

In every town or city, certain places are set aside for voting. These are called **polling places**, or polls. They may be in a school, a firehouse, or some other place that's easy to reach.

The polls open early in the morning on election day. They usually close at about 8 p.m. that night.

If you are registered to vote, you can find out where your polling place is by calling the registrar of voters at your town or city hall. The registrar has a list of all the voters in his or her city or town. The list shows where each voter should go to vote.

Ballots

In some towns and cities, voting is done by hand. The voter is given a ballot. A ballot is a card or sheet of paper with the names of the people running for office.

With some ballots, the voter marks an **X** next to the name of each person he or she wants to elect. With other ballots, the voter punches a hole in the card next to the name of each person he or she chooses.

Once the voter has finished marking the ballot, he or she drops it into a box. After the polls close, election officials open the ballot boxes. Then they count the votes for each person on the ballot.

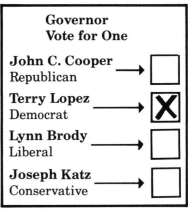

Governor
Vote for One

John C. Cooper Republican →	☐
Terry Lopez Democrat →	X
Lynn Brody Liberal →	☐
Joseph Katz Conservative →	☐

With this kind of ballot, the voter marks an X to show his or her choice.

With this kind of ballot, the voter punches a hole in a card to show his or her choice.

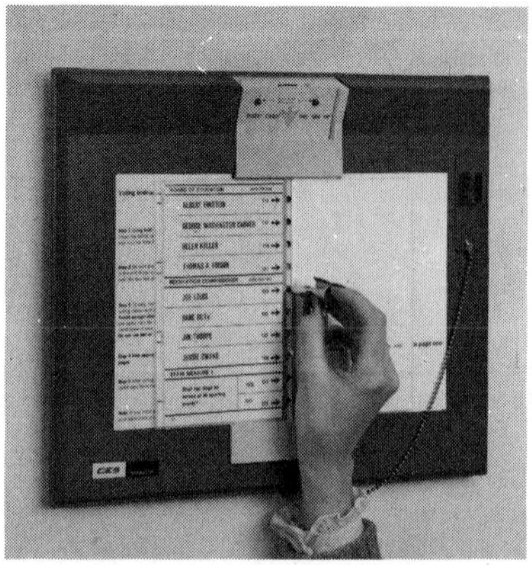

Computer Election Systems

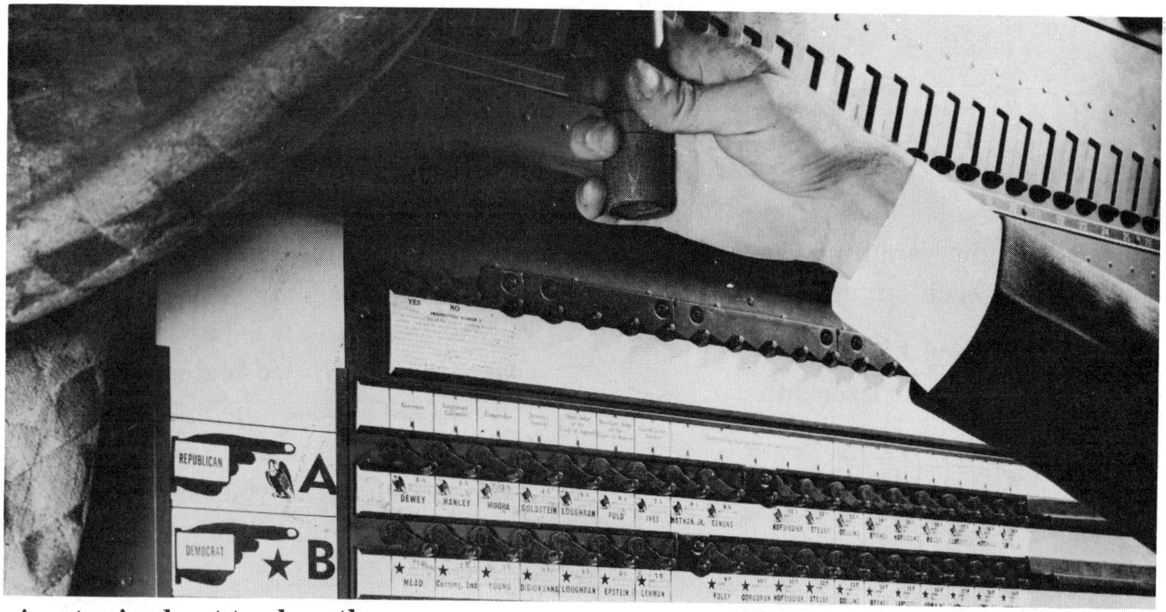

UPI/Bettmann Newsphotos

A voter is about to close the curtain of the voting machine. What do you think he will then do to choose the people he wants to elect?

Voting Machines

Many towns and cities use voting machines instead of ballots. Here's how the machines work.

- You step inside a little booth and close the curtain.
- You look over the names of all the people running for election.
- You pull down a small lever over the name of each person you want to elect.
- You open the curtain. When you do that, the machine records your vote. The levers you pulled down pop back up. And the machine is ready for the next voter.

Keeping Things Fair and Secret

At all polling places, voting is secret. No one can see whom you vote for. No one can force you to vote for a particular person.

Who makes sure that the voting is kept fair and secret? Election officials do. The officials make sure no one tries to keep people from voting. They also make sure that each person votes only once.

Informed Citizen

Facts First

Choose the right word from the Word List to complete each sentence below.

Word List

ballots	citizenship
register	secret
citizen	polling
levers	

1. In order to vote in elections, you must be at least 18 years old and a ________________ of the United States.
2. New voters must go to the office of their town or city clerk and ________________ to vote.
3. On election day, voters do their voting at special ________________ places.
4. In some towns and cities, voters mark ________________ to show whom they want to elect.
5. With a voting machine, you use small ________________ to select the people you want to elect.
6. Election officials make sure the voting is fair and ________________.
7. If you are not now a citizen of the United States, you can become one. Then you will get a set of ________________ papers.

Beyond the Facts

Here are some questions to think and talk about.

1. Why do you think it is important for citizens of the United States to vote?
2. Why do you suppose the law says that you have to be at least 18 years old and a citizen before you can vote?
3. Why is it important that voting be secret?

Close to Home

Here are some things you might like to do.

1. If you do not have a copy of your birth certificate, ask your teacher what you have to do to get one.
2. Register to vote, if you are at least 18 years old and a citizen of the United States.
3. If you are not a citizen of the United States, and would like to become one, ask your teacher to help you.
4. Call or visit the registrar of voters at your town or city hall. Find out if your town or city uses ballots or voting machines. See if you can have someone visit your school to show how to use the ballots or voting machines. Prepare a list of questions to ask about voting.

Glossary

Part 1
Congress, the President, and the Courts

Introduction

government, p. 8 The system and the people that run a town, city, county, state, or nation.

Unit 1: What Does Government Do?

control, p. 10 Direct or be in charge of.

department, p. 12 A part of a government or a business. The group of people who work there.

enforce, p. 13 Make sure that a rule or an order is followed.

informed citizen, p. 14 A citizen is a person who belongs to the U.S. by being born there, or by having at least one parent who is a citizen, or by passing the citizenship test. An informed citizen must know what is going on in government.

laws, p. 13 Rules made by a government.

license, p. 11 A government form that shows that a person or business has a special skill and has the government's permission to use it. There are licenses for doctors, drivers, pilots, plumbers, and teachers, to name a few.

obey, p. 13 Follow rules and laws.

police officer, p. 10 A person with the job of keeping law and order.

property, p. 12 The things that people own, like houses, cars, and furniture.

protect, p. 11 Guard or keep away from harm.

provide, p. 12 Give something that is needed.

referee, p. 13 The person who decides whether or not the players are following the rules of a game.

speed limits, p. 10 The fastest speeds that governments allow for motor vehicles, such as cars, trucks, and buses. Speed limit signs tell drivers how fast they can go.

traffic, p. 9 Motor vehicles moving along a street, road, or highway.

Unit 2: Where Is Government Found?

armed forces, p. 18 The parts of the military: army, navy, air force, and marines.

capital, p. 18 A city that is the center of government. Lawmakers work there. A capitol is the building in the capital city where the lawmakers do their work.

coins, p. 18 Makes metal money. Pennies, dimes, and other kinds of metal money are also called coins.

county, p. 16 A part of a state that has its own government. In some states, counties are called townships, boroughs, or parishes.

districts, p. 19 Areas in a city, state, or nation that have a special purpose, like water, fire and school districts.

District of Columbia (D.C.), p. 22 The special district that is not part of any state, where the national capital is located.

levels, p. 18 Parts of something that can be compared. The three levels of government are local, state, and national.

local, p. 15 About places that are smaller than a country or state: counties, cities, or towns.

nation, p. 16 Another word for country.

national, p. 15 About a whole nation or country.

permits, p. 20 Local government forms that allow people to do special things. Usually it's against the law to do these things without a permit. For example, you must get a permit before you can build a house.

protection, p. 19 Safety from danger or defense against attack.

state, p. 15 One of the 50 parts of the United States that has its own government.

taxes, p. 20 The money that citizens pay to a government. Taxes help pay the costs of running the government and providing services.

Unit 3: Who Set Up Our Government?

article, p. 28 A separate part of a written plan. One of the seven parts of the United States Constitution.

Constitution of the United States, p. 28 The plan for our national government. It tells how our country's laws should be made and carried out, and by whom. It also tells what the government can and cannot do.

delegates, p. 26 People chosen by groups to speak for them.

federal, p. 27 In a federal system of government, all the states agree that the national government will be stronger than the state governments. The states agree to obey national laws.

powers, p. 28 The things a government can do under its law.

rights, p. 28 Things that people have and can do that are named and protected by a government's constitution.

tax collector, p. 24 A government employee who supervises the department that collects tax money.

Unit 4: How Is Power Kept in Check?

branch, p. 31 A part of something. One of the three parts of government. (See the definitions of *Congress, executive, judicial,* and *legislative* below.)

cases of law, p. 34 Matters for the courts to decide.

Congress, p. 32 The legislative, or lawmaking, branch of the national government. It is made up of the Senate and the House of Representatives.

crimes, p. 34 The things people do that break laws.

defend, p. 34 Keep safe or protect.

disputes, p. 31 Arguments between people, businesses, or governments, usually about laws, rights, property, or money.

executive, p. 31 About being in charge of the affairs of a government, a business, or an organization. The name of the branch of government that takes care of running a nation, state, or city. An executive is the person who is in charge.

House of Representatives, p. 32 One of the two parts (or houses) of Congress. The House of Representatives has many more members than the Senate because the Constitution says there must be one representative for every 30 thousand people in a state.

judicial, p. 31 About deciding on cases of law. The name of the branch of government that studies and decides on court cases for a nation, state, or city.

jury, p. 34 A group of twelve people chosen in a court of law to decide on a case.

legislative, p. 31 About making laws. The name of the branch of government that makes laws for a nation, state, or city.

preserve, p. 34 Keep something from changing.

President, p. 33 The top executive of our nation. A president is also the top executive of a business or an organization.

representatives, p. 32 The men and women who are chosen by the people to work in the House of Representatives.

Senate, p. 32 One of the two parts (or houses) of Congress. The Senate has two members from each state who are chosen by the people.

senators, p. 32 The men and women who are chosen by the people to work in the Senate.

separate, p. 31 Divide something into parts.

treaties, p. 34 Agreements made between nations.

trials, p. 31 The way government tests the facts of a case in a court of law. Trials are held to decide whether or not laws have been broken.

two-thirds, p. 33 Two out of every three. A two-thirds vote is needed in both the Senate and the House of Representatives to pass a bill the President doesn't sign.

Unit 5: What Are the People's Rights?

amendments, p. 37 Changes in something that correct it or make it better. Additions made to the Constitution.

assemble, p. 38 Get together with other people for a meeting.

bail, p. 39 Money an accused person must pay the court as a promise that he or she will come back for trial.

Bill of Rights, p. 36 The first ten amendments to the Constitution that guarantee our personal rights. Freedom of religion and the right to assemble are two of these personal rights.

guilty, p. 39 Proven wrong or deserving to be punished for breaking a law.

judges, p. 39 The people who listen to and decide on cases in courts of law.

lawyer, p. 39 A person who has studied the law and works to help people solve their legal problems.

press (the), p. 38 Newspapers, magazines, radio, television, and the people who work for them. The Bill of Rights guarantees a free press in this country.

religion, p. 38 A system of believing in and worshiping a divine or superhuman power. The Bill of Rights guarantees freedom of religion to all people in this country.

speech, p. 38 The act of talking or saying words aloud. The Bill of Rights guarantees that all Americans have freedom of speech.

under arrest, p. 36 Be stopped and held by the police under the law.

warrant, p. 39 A form signed by a judge that gives the police permission to search a home or arrest a person.

Unit 6: What Makes a Democracy?

democracy, p. 43 Government by the people. Government in which the people make the laws and decisions, or else they choose others to represent them in doing this.

direct, p. 43 By the shortest way, with nothing or no one in between.

elections, p. 44 The times when people choose their leaders and lawmakers by vote.

majority, p. 44 The larger number. In an election, how many *more* votes the winning side got than the losing side.

minority, p. 45 The smaller number. In an election, how many *fewer* votes the losing side got than the winning side. A smaller group of people is also called a minority. For example, black people and old people are both minority groups.

voters, p. 43 Citizens who choose their government leaders by picking the people they want in an election.

Unit 7: How Do People Get Elected?

ballot, p. 51 A card or sheet of paper that lists the names of the people who want to get elected to government jobs. Voters make their choices by marking names on the ballot.

candidate, p. 50 A person who is trying to get elected to a government job. A candidate is said to be running for a government job.

convention, p. 51 A big meeting to choose the candidates who will run in an election for government jobs.

elected, p. 48 Chosen by the vote of the people.

political party, p. 49 A group of people who share beliefs about government. Members of a political party work together to help their leaders and lawmakers get elected.

primary election, p. 51 A vote to choose a political party's candidates.

public office, p. 49 A general name for government jobs. People who are candidates for government jobs are said to be "running for public office."

Vice-President, p. 50 The person who is just below the President and who can take the President's place when needed.

Unit 8: How Does Congress Work?

agriculture, p. 57 Farming.

bills, p. 55 Written plans for laws that are presented to Congress.

committees, p. 57 Groups of people who work together to find out something, solve a problem, or get a job done.

debate, p. 55 Argue for or against something.

hearing, p. 57 A meeting to hear arguments for and against something.

lobbyists, p. 58 People who work for special-interest groups, like farmers or automakers. Lobbyists try to get laws passed that help their own groups.

majority leader, p. 55 A senator chosen to lead the other senators from the political party that has the larger number of members in the Senate.

majority party, p. 56 The political party that has the larger number of members in the Senate or the House of Representatives.

minority party, p. 56 The political party that has the smaller number of members in the Senate or the House of Representatives.

opinions, p. 57 Beliefs or feelings about something.

pass, p. 57 Approve a law by vote.

program, p. 58 A plan of action to make something better or solve a problem.

Speaker of the House, p. 55 A representative chosen by the other representatives from the political party that has a majority in the House. It is the job of the Speaker to lead the meetings in the House of Representatives.

specialize, p. 57 Know most about and work at one particular thing.

staff, p. 56 A group of workers who help their boss get the job done.

Unit 9: How Do Bills Become Laws?

environment, p. 61 Everything around us. Some of the environment is natural —for example, the woods and lakes and the wildlife that lives in them. Some of the environment is made by people—for example, cities and dams.

pocket veto, p. 64 The President can defeat a bill by not signing it before Congress ends its work for the year. This is called a pocket veto.

pollution, p. 60 All the things that make the environment dirty and unhealthy.

subcommittee, p. 62 A small group chosen from the larger committee to work on a special job. The subcommittee reports on its work to the committee.

veto, p. 64 Defeat or stop a bill from becoming a law. The President vetoes a bill by sending it back to Congress with a letter saying why he won't sign it. Or the President may use the pocket veto.

Unit 10: What Does the President Do?

budget, p. 67 A plan for spending money.

chief executive, p. 67 The head of the executive branch of a government or an organization. The president is the chief executive of the national government.

emergencies, p. 67 Sudden happenings that call for quick action.

missiles, p. 68 Rocket bombs that can hit targets far away.

relations, p. 67 The way persons, groups, or governments feel and act toward each other.

sworn, p. 66 Having made a solemn promise or taken an oath to do something. A President has sworn to work for the good of the country.

weapons, p. 68 Guns, tanks, missiles, and other equipment used for fighting wars.

Unit 11: Who Works for the President?

agencies, p. 73 Groups who work for a larger organization and specialize in one thing. There are about 1200 agencies in the national government.

appointed, p. 76 Picked out for a job in government. For example, the members of the cabinet are appointed by the President.

cabinet, p. 76 The heads of the 13 national executive departments who serve as advisors to the President.

FBI, p. 73 The Federal Bureau of Investigation. This government agency gathers information about people who break national laws.

IRS, p. 73 The Internal Revenue Service. This government agency collects taxes for the government.

OMB, p. 73 The Office of Management and Budget. This special executive group helps the President plan the federal budget.

secretary, p. 76 A person in charge of a department of government, like the Secretary of Agriculture.

Unit 12: Who Pays for Government?

deduct, p. 79 Take out or subtract.

duties, p. 81 The name of taxes the national government charges on goods that come into the United States from other countries. Another name for import taxes.

excise, p. 80 The name of taxes the national government charges on certain goods and services.

import, p. 81 The name of taxes the national government charges on goods that come into the United States from other countries. Another name for duties. *Import* also means to bring goods into the United States from another country.

income, p. 79 The name of taxes governments charge people and businesses on the money they earn. *Income* also means the money earned by people and businesses.

interest, p. 82 The extra money a person has to pay a bank for getting a loan. The bank charges interest on the loan amount, and the person has to pay back the loan amount plus the interest.

revenue, p. 79 All the money that a government collects in different ways.

Unit 13: What Do the Courts Do?

appeal, p. 88 Ask that a court case be reviewed by a higher court in order to try to get a different decision.

civil, p. 86 About a citizen's rights, duties, or affairs.

contracts, p. 86 Agreements to do business.

criminal, p. 85 About breaking the law. A criminal is a person who breaks the law.

customs, p. 84 The government agency that collects the taxes a government charges people who bring goods in and out of the country. Sometimes *customs* also means the taxes themselves.

defendant, p. 85 A person accused of a crime who is on trial.

evidence, p. 85 Facts given during a trial.

fees, p. 86 Money charged for services or for the right to do something. Lawyers charge fees to defend people. States charge fees to register and drive a car.

illegal, p. 84 Against the law.

inspector, p. 84 A person with the job of looking at something closely to see if it is all right.

officials, p. 87 People who are in charge of public departments or who have important government jobs.

reverse, p. 88 Turn something around so that it is the opposite of what it was.

small claims court, p. 86 A civil court of law that usually handles cases involving less than $1500.

sue, p. 86 Take a person, group, or business to court to settle problems and try to get money for something done to you.

verdict, p. 85 The decision of the jury: guilty or not guilty.

Unit 14: Why Is the Supreme Court Special?

draft, p. 93 A government order for people to work in the armed forces. People must obey a draft order whether they want to or not.

gavel, p. 90 A light hammer that a judge or other official uses to bang on a table to get people's attention.

guardian, p. 92 A person or organization that takes charge of something and keeps it safe.

justices, p. 90 The nine judges of the Supreme Court.

Unit 15: Is the Constitution Still Working?

boycotted, p. 99 Refused to buy, sell, or use something as a sign that you don't like what's going on.

confession, p. 97 Admitting guilt.

ERA, p. 100 Equal Rights Amendment. This proposed constitutional amendment says that women must be given equal rights under the law.

NOW, p. 100 National Organization of Women. This group was formed in the 1960s to help women win equality with men.

register, p. 99 Sign up to vote. People must register in order to be able to vote.

segregation, p. 99 The separation of one group from the rest of the people. In this country, black people were often segregated in schools, public places, and neighborhoods.

Part 2
From City Hall to State Capitol

Unit 16: What Are Local Laws About?

damages, p. 106 Money a person has to pay, under the law, to make up for something done to someone else or to property.

disturbing the peace, p. 107 Bothering other people, such as by making loud noise or blocking streets.

officers, p. 106 People who have jobs with decision-making power in government or business.

responsible, p. 106 Having an obligation or duty to do something.

signals, p. 109 Signs that tell when to do something. A red traffic signal is a sign to stop.

trespassing, p. 108 Going onto someone's land or property without permission.

vandalism, p. 108 Damage done on purpose to things that belong to someone else.

Unit 17: Who Makes Local Laws?

ban, p. 114 Stop something from being done, sold, or used, and make it against the law.

city council, p. 112 The group that makes city laws and decides on how the city should be run.

rush hours, p. 115 The hours between 7 and 9 in the morning and 5 and 7 at night when people are going to and leaving work. Traffic is very heavy during these times, and local governments often make laws to control it.

Unit 18: Who Runs Local Government?

clinics, p. 120 Places where people can get free or low-cost medical care. The health department of the local government often runs clinics in a city or town.

commissioners, p. 119 The heads of public departments, like the fire and police departments in a city or town.

library, p. 120 A public building where people can go to use or borrow books, records, tapes, and other materials.

mayor, p. 117 The chief executive in a city or town government.

planning, p. 120 The name of a department in local government that directs how a city or town grows.

public works, p. 120 The name of a department in local government that builds and cares for the streets and public buildings in a city or town.

recreation, p. 121 The name of a department in local government that builds and runs city and town parks, community centers, playgrounds, and swimming pools.

sanitation, p. 121 The name of a department in local government that keeps a city or town clean and healthy.

superintendent, p. 119 A person whose job is to take care of the day-to-day activities of a group. For example, the superintendent of schools is in charge of running the schools in a city or town.

transportation, p. 121 The name of a department in local government that runs the city or town buses, ferries, and subways.

welfare, p. 121 The name of a department in local government that helps people with no income meet their needs for food, clothing, shelter, and medical care.

Unit 19: What Do Local Courts Do?

charge, p. 124 The crime a person is accused of in a court of law.

divorce, p. 127 The ending of a marriage under the laws of the state.

files, p. 125 Puts a legal paper into the public record.

justice of the peace, p. 127 A person elected by the voters of a town to do certain things under the law. A justice of the peace may listen and decide on traffic and other kinds of local cases and perform wedding ceremonies.

juvenile, p. 127 About young people. The name of a local court that handles cases involving people under 18 years old who are accused of breaking law.

legal separation, p. 127 A legal agreement that married people make to live apart.

minors, p. 127 In most states, people who are under 18 years old, or juveniles.

plead, p. 124 Tell the court if you're guilty or not guilty of the charge made against you.

versus, p. 124 Against.

witnesses, p. 125 People who see something happen and tell about it later in court.

Unit 20: What Are State Laws About?

consent, p. 131 An OK, an agreement, or permission given to do something.

fund, p. 130 Money set aside for a special purpose. Both workers and employers pay into the state unemployment fund.

unemployment, p. 130 Being without a job. Also, the name of the state insurance that pays certain people who are out of work while they are looking for new jobs.

workers' compensation, p. 129 Money people receive after getting hurt so badly on the job that they need to take time off. Both workers and employers pay into the state workers' compensation fund.

Unit 21: Who Makes State Laws?

governor, p. 136 The chief executive in state government.

introduced, p. 136 Started or brought in for the first time.

legislature, p. 135 The lawmaking part of a government.

Unit 22: Who Runs State Governments?

attorney general, p. 143 The chief lawyer for a state or a nation.

benefits, p. 145 Payments made to people by an insurance company or a government agency. Benefits include unemployment insurance and workers' compensation.

colleges, p. 144 Schools for students who want to continue their education after high school. Colleges may offer two-year certificate programs and four-year degree programs. Some colleges also have short programs to help students in their work or life that take much less time than two years to finish.

disasters, p. 142 Floods, fires, or other major problems that hurt people and destroy their property.

issues, p. 143 Gives or sends out.

legal advisor, p. 143 A person with the job of helping others understand the law and how the courts work.

lieutenant, p. 143 A person who acts in the place of someone who is higher up. In state government, the lieutenant governor is in charge when the governor is away.

pardon, p. 142 Forgive and release from punishment.

propose, p. 142 Suggest.

research, p. 144 Careful study of something to find out how it works and how it can help people. For example, medical research has found cures and medicines for many illnesses.

riots, p. 142 Large crowds of people making noisy public disturbances. People can be hurt and property destroyed during a riot.

term, p. 142 A certain length of time. A governor usually serves a term of four years.

tie vote, p. 143 The same number of people vote for and against a bill. Sometimes there is a tie vote for candidates running for a government job.

treasurer, p. 143 A person in charge of money. In government, the treasurer is often the tax collector and handles all the money that goes in and out of the treasury.

universities, p. 144 Schools for advanced education after high school. Universities offer four-year degree programs and other advanced degrees that may take many years of study to finish. They have great libraries and laboratories in which students do major research in such areas as science, medicine, education, and electronics.

Unit 23: What Do State Courts Do?

complaint, p. 149 A charge against someone or something that is made in a court of law.

cross-examine, p. 148 The way lawyers in court question each other's witnesses in order to check the answers to earlier questions.

defense, p. 148 In a court case, the side for the accused person who is on trial. The defense lawyer tries to get the court to drop the charges against the defendant.

lawsuit, p. 149 The case resulting when someone sues another person or organization and takes them to court.

plaintiff, p. 149 The person who makes the charge against the accused person in a court of law.

prosecution, p. 148 In a court case, the side against the accused person who is on trial. The prosecution lawyer tries to prove that the defendant is guilty of the charges.

Unit 24: Who Pays the Bills?

meters, p. 155 Instruments for measuring the amount of something. A parking meter measures the amount of time you can use a parking space by the amount of money you put into the meter.

toll, p. 157 Money a state or local government collects from drivers for using certain highways, bridges, and tunnels.

zone, p. 155 Spaces along streets and roads that have special uses under the law. Some examples are loading zones, no parking zones, no truck zones, and tow-away zones.

Unit 25: How Do You Become a Voter?

birth certificate, p. 160 A government form that tells when and where a person was born and who the parents were.

convicted, p. 160 Found or proven guilty of a crime by a court of law.

polling places, p. 162 Places set aside for voting. Schools and fire stations are often used as polling places.

registrar, p. 160 A person with the job of signing up, or registering, people to vote.

registration, p. 160 Signing up to vote by filling in your name and other facts about yourself on a special form.

Vocabulary

Index
Our Government in Action